CELEBRATING
B.A. SRIRANGAMMA

The Pioneer of Women's Education

- SUJAYA S. BHAGAWAN -

ISBN 979-8-89067-822-5

Contents

In Loving Memory:

Of our dear late Mother and wife, Sujaya Sheshadri Bhagawan. She worked tirelessly and passionately on this book of tales, which she so fondly used to tell my friends and I, and all of our family members about the great B.A. Srirangamma! It was her last wish to publish this story and we were finally able to make this happen. I love you, Mom.

– Shreyus Bhagawan and Venkatesha Bhagawan

Foreword

This is a heartwarming story of a grandmother written with enormous gratitude by a grand daughter. The grandmother, Smt. Srirangamma, comes across as a compassionate, courageous, dedicated and a rather experimental person in the loving eyes of her granddaughter, Smt. Sujaya Bhagawan.

The grandmother, being the first woman graduate of the erstwhile princely Mysore state obviously makes her a pioneer with a ready place in history. But, it is not just Smt. Srirangamma's personal advancement through a liberal arts degree in early 20th century that the author finds fascinating. The focus is on her larger personality, which not just advances her family's path but continuously nudges the progress of a larger society.

Therefore, this writing is not just a slice of personal history but endeavours to find a quiet spot in the history of women's education and empowerment in British India. It simultaneously illustrates and reiterates the benevolent and visionary attributes of the Mysore Wodeyars, who envisioned a progressive and modern state. Interestingly and coincidentally, Srirangamma's educational success happens when Mysore state is being presided over by a queen regent. She takes immense pride and celebrates Srirangamma's trailblazing efforts. The patriarchal mould had been broken and the glass ceiling had been shattered under the queen regent's watchful eyes — a rare moment of sisterhood.

As much as the grandmother's trials are listed in this short piece of writing, in the backdrop is the early tragedy of the author herself. She is orphaned young and is thrust into care of her grandmother, who puts her on an enriching and sustaining path of life. The author's survival and success itself becomes testimony to the grandmother's trust and vision.

I wish Smt. Sujaya Bhagawan was alive to see the fruits of her labour. She was passionate about recording her tribute to her grandmother. I have also personally experienced the warmth and hospitality of Kusuma Bhavan, the quaintly palatial home that Smt. Srirangamma built in the early decades of the 20th century, albeit in another time and from another occupant of the house. For many years after 2000, I used to frequent the house to spend long hours talking to one of India's finest documentary filmmakers — MV Krishnaswamy. He was a son-in-law of the house. His wife and Smt. Sujaya Bhagawan were cousins. Krishnaswamy belonged to a very talented Mysore generation that included cartoonist RK Laxman, photographer TS Satyan, sociologist MN Srinivas, and Indira Gandhi's trusted aide, HY Sharada Prasad.

The physical presence of Kusuma Bhavan, which no longer exists, defined the character of an entire Bangalore locality — Malleswaram, and the intellectual life it offered was unparalleled. We should all be thankful to Smt. Sujaya Bhagawan for keeping memories alive by discussing the life and work of Kusuma Bhavan's matriarch.

– Sugata Srinivasaraju
May 2024

Testimonials About Srirangamma From Friends and Family

"My home would immediately become spirited because of Akkaya's (Srirangamma) arrival, to visit her sister in Mysore. She would assert herself, and preside over the household affairs.

The sisters would enthusiastically exchange recipes and discuss the finer aspects of culinary expertise, like tempering, seasoning, and presentation of the Srivaishnava specialities like *Rasam*. Akkaya acknowledged her sister's special talent in cooking certain delicacies such as *Kadambam*, a modification of *Bisi Bele Bhath*.

According to Pandith Rajeev Tatanath, Srirangamma's house was a hub of intellectual discussions. It was like a Parisian intellectual salon, where distinguished thinkers, budding writers, musicians, and artists met periodically."

– Professor M.N. Panini

"I recall the days when I had the privilege of watching Srirangamma sitting majestically in the armchair, her commanding voice enunciating words in impeccable English.

As a little girl, visiting my cousins during the school holidays, I was not aware of her reputation or fame. Srirangamma certainly had a royal commanding aura about her. I always felt a regal presence at her home in Kusum Bhavan, whenever she was around."

– Ms. Prabha Prasad

"I met Srirangamma in Bombay, and was fascinated by Suji's elderly Grandma, who wore a traditional saree and spoke immaculate posh English! I invited her to my home."

– Mira Mehta

Srirangamma was so simple that she visited and met Mira's father, Gijubhai. He was respectful and hospitable to her. She told him that she was pleased to meet his bubbly, happy-go-lucky daughter. She expressed that she was happy about their friendship which could be mutually beneficial. Mira could be her pen pal, as Suji was good at letter writing. Gijubhai blessed both the girls and permitted Mira to accompany her to visit her friends.

On the visit, Mira was impressed at how relaxed and comfortable Grandma was, as she spontaneously expressed her unbiased and honest views when she was requested to participate in the host's family affairs. Srirangamma had the sophisticated response of a gentle, educated cultured elder, who strongly influenced the teen Mira!

"When they visited Grandma's other friend, Laxmi Bai, she seemed even more relaxed. She enjoyed being jovial. Her interactions were so natural, that her good sense of humour was obvious."

"Srirangamma was a good friend of my mother Sumathi Ammal. My mother was a graduate and daughter of great lawyer of Madras Jnanasambandam. Srirangamma was very much influenced by Taranath. She used to be the host to great personalities like Bellary Ragaavachari, T P Kailasam and Pt. Taranath. She was a well read and dignified woman and initiated numerous intellectual discussions at her house. She always welcomed intellectuals of her day. She herself was active in her own right. I remember spending really long hours at Srirangamma's house Kusuma Bhavan in the company of my father or mother as a young boy of 10/11. I remember seeing several pencil sketches of women drawn by her daughter-in-law Sarojamma (Kitta's wife, if I am correct) in the drawing room of Srirangamma.

She was a great patron of art and artists—though she was not super rich, she was generous in her support to art and artists. While other women of her times lazed out their time idly, she was active and had continuous interaction with the leading luminaries of her day. She pioneered in girls' education; she rejected traditions, customs that exploited women. She was completely against Indian treatment of woman. She wanted to uplift Indian women from the morass of superstitions and exploitation. Of course, she had to face challenges of orthodoxy prevailing among her relatives; she did extremely well in facing these challenges. She was extremely kind to her guests – I still remember the hospitality offered by her to us. I as a teenager spent more time at her house. Her house ever welcomed worthy guests. I remember her as a lady ahead of her times – striving to get as many as possible girls enrolled in the school. She travelled across the state in her car. She held high position in the government education department. Srirangamma was a pioneer in her field."

– Pandith Rajeev Taranath

"One morning we Swamy's got the news of our grandmother's demise, in the village. The day's cooking was already done, for the day. Our mother, Susheela Swamy was busy, on the phone.

At noon my brother and I got ready to set the table, and warmed up the food, and to serve the guests, since our mother was distraught and busy.

We both were oblivious of the taboo that a grieving family is not to entertain or feed guests. or that the orthodox guests do not expect or accept hospitality by the family in grief!

When invited, to the table, Srirangamma first thought that we were playing pranks, daring to serve food to her! But she was quick to understand our innocent and yet genuine gesture. She did not get offended, explained and advised us gracefully.

In good humour, she sought our help to catch a local train, to relocate to another friend's house, in the city."

– Professor Vijay Swamy, and his brother Vasant were teens, when Srirangamma was once visiting them, for her annual participation in All India Women's Conference, in Pune.

Srirangamma, The Mysore Celebrity

This story is special because my paternal grandmother was a true pioneer of women's education in the state of Mysore, at the dawn of the 20th century.

Amba (as I fondly addressed my grandmother), had earned a coveted place in the history of women's education, by virtue of being the very first woman to earn a B.A. Degree. She scripted history by graduating as a pioneer from the Cradle of Education, Mysore.

Mahatma Gandhiji once said, "Woman is the noblest of God's creation, Supreme in her sphere of society." Amba was indeed a celebrity of her time, in the early 20th century. Can you guess what this actually means?

Maharani Kempananjammanni, the Queen Reagent, and wife of Sri Chmarajendra Wodeyar, and the mother of His Highness, Krishna Raja Wodeyar, summoned Sow. Srirangamma to the palace. She personally congratulated Srirangamma for her exemplary achievement and gave orders for this young lady pioneer to be sent on a procession in the royal coach around Mysore city.

By then, some of Amba's relatives, family and friends, out of their own ignorance and narrow outlook, had severed connections with Amba, looking down upon her for having defied established norms. According to them, Srirangamma had taken the unthinkable, unpardonable lead to pursue her undergraduate studies among men, at the all-men's Central College in Bangalore!

They had already taken the liberty to spread vile rumours and boycotted Srirangamma's entire family. Many of them openly refused to stay in touch.

However, such profound recognition by none other than the royal family gradually made people stop and think. When they observed what a grand welcome, and great honour Srirangamma, (my Amba) had received from the entire royal family and the elite of Mysore, it dawned on the naysayers that they had stooped down to an unbecoming level of thinking.

It made them wonder if there could actually be something special about this young lady who was in fact the first woman to complete her college education in Mysore. People's attitudes gradually started changing towards education in general, and the young lady in particular. Eventually, there was a 360-degree change!

Amba became known as 'B. A. Srirangamma' and she became popular in every household in Mysore and Bangalore.

Pioneers of Women's Education in Mysore

(1903-1906)

Sow. Srirangamma, Sow. K.D. Rukmaniamma and Sow. Subbamma completed their high school education in 1896. They were the first three girls to graduate from Maharani's High School.

My grandmother, Amba, was a distinguished student. She was advised to pursue her collegiate education at Central College, Bangalore, by the royal family in Mysore, and Diwan Rangacharlu, who was in office at the time. (Review of Progress Of Education In Mysore State 1911-1916, p137).

When Sow. Srirangamma and her aunt, Sow. K.D. Rukmaniamma completed their B.A. Degree, it was announced in 1906 by the Madras Presidency. This was a landmark in the history of women's education, in Mysore. They were both invited to the Mysore Palace personally and congratulated by the Maharani for being distinguished graduates in the State of Mysore. of Maharani's College.

Other upcoming female students were influenced by the pioneers. In 1908, Subbamma, a lady student, passed the Mysore Panditha's exam for the first time in Kannada.

Indiramma was the first woman to graduate among the *Vokkaligas* (labour class). She completed a Diploma in Education, and M.A. in Adult Education from Leads University, London, in 1928.

Graduation Ceremonies and Congratulatory Celebrations

There was indeed a profuse spirit of congratulations and celebrations all over Mysore city and the state when the Madras Presidency announced the graduation of these pioneering ladies! Srirangamma and K.D. Rukmaniamma were the first women graduates of Mysore, as previously mentioned. Srirangamma passed her degree with a First Class and in second place. Her subjects were Kannada, English and History. Each year one subject was to be completed. Science, History, Geography, and English had to be studied in the third year.

Rukmaniamma completed her B.A. Degree from Maharani's College, Mysore, after Maharani's High School was upgraded to a second-grade college in 1902.

Both the outstanding women graduates received congratulations and *khillaths* (tokens of appreciation as gifts) from the Maharani Regent Kempanamjammanni at the Mysore palace. Srirangamma received a *thoda* (bracelet) studded with gems and the royal emblem of Ganda Berunda. Rukmaniamma received a gorgeous tissue saree gifted to her on an engraved silver platter.

Amba elaborated on their graduation ceremony in Madras. At the convocation, it was quite a rare sight in the Madras Senate House to see every graduate walking up to the Governor in their cap and gown!

Thousands of people gave Srirangamma a standing ovation for more than 10 minutes, starting from when she rose from her seat, till she returned to it.

There was a grand dinner that followed. She and Rukmaniamma were the only two graduates from Mysore. Amba received many presents and thoroughly enjoyed the special entertainment.

The Mylapore Association of Madras also entertained the pioneers, with Lady Benson presiding over it. Besides festoons and speeches, they presented her with a silver casket, and blouse material. Mrs. Swaminathan and her sister hosted the evening entertainment.

The Prince and Princess of Wales also attended the event at the Presidency in 1906. Srirangamma was introduced to them in an interview. She got to shake hands with the Prince and Princess.

They asked if she was married, and had any children. She told them that she had four children and showed them a picture of her wards.

"Very jolly!" the Princess exclaimed. "It's a wonder! How do you manage?"

Srirangamma mentioned that her mother was with her to help, besides the domestic help and the support of her in-laws.

Srirangamma and K.D. Rukmaniamma were photographed together in their graduation gowns. The former then posed with her brother, Sri Varadhan, who was also in his gown. He graduated from law school the same year (1906) from Bangalore Law College.

Srirangamma sounded so excited when she told everyone that she had mailed her graduation photos to her friends in various parts of India.

Srirangamma's Family Background and Early Childhood

I would like to share with you the exciting story of an extraordinary person, Srirangamma. Her life was full of dynamic changes, incredible challenges, and adventure. Therefore, it was highly eventful.

Do you know why her story is so special? It's because she was an incredible path-breaker, and she dared to defy ancient norms. She dared to take strides against established social norms, to bring about a change in the way people thought, especially about what women are truly capable of.

She was the first lady to have graduated from The Cradle of Education in the state of Mysore, making history. Further, her life was a shining example of a truly emancipated woman, when life was much more difficult more than a century ago.

Srirangamma surely paved the way for women of the late 19th and early 20th centuries to break social barriers and enter the educational arena. This is the story of this iconic personality. It is a testimony of her achievements throughout her eventful life.

She came from humble beginnings. Her parents worked in the Adiranga Temple in Srirangapatna, 18 kilometres north of Mysore city. Her father, Kavi Gopalachar, was the son of Kavi (poet) Varadachar, who was the Aasthan Kavi (court poet) during the reign of Krishna Raja Wodayar III of Mysore. Her mother, Ambuja, was the daughter of Sri Sheshachar and Sow Laxmi, who had migrated from Srirangam in Tiruchirapalli district to Mysore, walking through the forests!

They were Srivaishnava Brahmins from the Tamil Iyengar community and were orthodox and conservative in their outlook and practice.

Srirangam's father, Gopalachar, suffered an early death, when her mother, Ambuja, was barely 18 years of age. She had to live under her mother Laxmi's protection with her three children in Bangalore. Her maternal uncle (*maama*), Ramaswamy Iyengar, and grandmother's brother, Ambil Narasimha Iyengar, generously supported Laxmi's entire family, both financially and emotionally.

Ambil Narasimha Iyengar (A.N.I) observed that young Srirangam was very bright and talented. He watched her play on the banks of the Kaveri River with wet sand and river pebbles, building sand castles and writing with her fingers on the wet sand. That's when he had first toyed with the idea of adopting her, aspiring to educate her.

Ambil Narasimha Iyengar discussed his wish to educate Srirangam with Ambujam. Her response was that she had plans for Srirangam's life. She wanted to get her daughter married when she was around 10 years or so, before it was too late! She suggested that he personally tutor her till she got married.

Vidhyarambham

Ambil Narasimha Iyengar was keen on adopting the little girl, Srirangam. He was committed to Ambuja, to help her find a suitable groom for the child.

He arranged a *Vidhyarambham* (initiation of formal learning) ceremony at his residence when Srirangam was about 8 years old. He invited only young girls in the neighbourhood. Among them were Sumangala, Kalyani, and Mangala Gowri. Most of the young teenagers were a few years older than Srirangam and were among the first students of Maharani's Girls School, which he had just established, despite incredible challenges.

Sumangala Kalyani, Shubha, and Mangala Gowri were teenage widows, who explained that since they were widows, they couldn't attend the celebration, as they were considered to be inauspicious.

According to traditional beliefs (taboos), widows usually had to be confined to the dark attics or basements, were given simple bland food, and could not indulge in feasts. They were not eligible to groom themselves, wear attractive outfits, or mingle with visitors.

Ambil Narasimha Iyengar was shocked to hear what the girls told him. He personally visited the neighbours and convinced the respective parents that the senior girls had the responsibility of teaching Srirangam to sing a song of prayer to Saraswathi (Goddess of Learning). He insisted that they attend the special celebration. He made sure that all the girls had the approval of their respective families. There were no arguments or compromises about it.

He exclusively spoke to the four girls about their auspicious names. He advised them to start identifying with the significance of their beautiful names. He convinced them to practice their normal routines. They were entitled to receive an education and were encouraged to shun superstitions and blind practices.

Srirangam's mother and grandmother sighed with relief that only children were invited. There were no adults to make comments, complain or gossip.

Srirangam pranced around happily in her new mini half saree. She wore the jingly, colourful bangles that her uncle had given her with blessings. Her mother had braided her long hair and decorated it with fragrant jasmine flowers.

Srirangam was presented with a framed picture of the dancing Saraswathi and a beautiful brass lamp. She was instructed to light the same with a wick and oil with her mother's help on all special occasions. There were white flowers, coloured roses, incense sticks and fruits neatly arranged on trays.

All the invitees received an earthen lamp each and were asked to light their lamps from the flame of Srirangam's brass lamp. The girls were full of smiles and were busy lighting their own lamps using the oil and wick. N. Iyengar enjoyed the symbolic practice of one flame lighting all the lamps.

Sumangali and Kalyani sang an invocation together. The Vidhyarambam Ceremony involved Srirangam writing the alphabets on grains including rice and wheat, dal, sugar, sand, turmeric, and Kumkum powder, that were placed on trays. They provided multi-sensory stimulation for the fingers.

Eventually, Narasimha Iyengar took his finger ring off and wrote the OUM sign on Srirangam's tongue, saying a lengthy OM into her ears!

The senior girls taught Srirangam to sing the Saraswathi Namasthubyam. The lyrics signified the student's appeal to Goddess Saraswathi. "I bow to you, the giver of boons! Please bless me with success, as I initiate the process of formal literacy and education!"

Ambil Narasimha Iyengar lifted little Srirangam up, cradled her in his arms, walked to the pooja room (alter) and said, "Lord Narayana, I am in the process of adopting this child for life, with the resolve to raise her with love, and educate her. Please help me in my resolve."

He was ecstatic on being successful in his *Dattu Sweekara Vidhi* (the ritual of accepting and undertaking adoption). Srirangam's mother Ambuja and her mother Laxmi cried tears of joy.

The new and excited father, Narasimha Iyengar, served the festive lunch to the young guests. Everyone enjoyed the delicious feast. All the girls were full of smiles, and were pleased to take home their lamps. Srirangam's mother Ambuja, grandmother Laxmi, and Ambil Narasimha Iyengar's family thanked the young guests for their help, and bid them farewell.

My great grandfather, Ambil Narasimha Iyengar, was determined to demystify the misconceptions surrounding young girls, especially widows, caused by taboo. His mission to invite only young girls and let them have a good time, free of prejudices, was accomplished!

Advent of Srirangamma's Schooling and Early Education

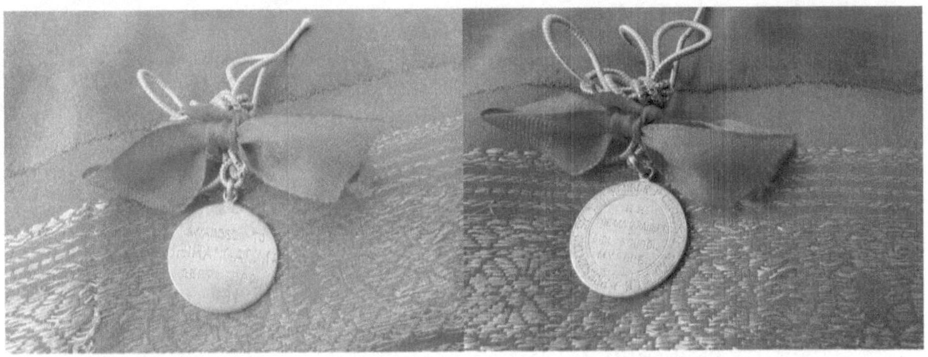

Maharani's Girls School, Maharani's High School, and Maharani's College was the dream child of A.N. Iyengar. It was established despite a host of challenges. Eventually, the two crusaders, A.N. Iyengar and his social reformer and journalist friend, Sri. M. Venkatakrishnaiah, succeeded in establishing the school in 1881. So, the movement of women's education was mobilised, to the joy of the crusaders.

My grandmother, Srirangam, was admitted in Grade 3 at Maharani's Girls School, when she was about 8 years old, around the year 1884. Her father was committed to finding a suitable groom for a rather young Srirangam. He found a young man who had plans to continue his collegiate education.

Young Srirangam was married when she had just turned 10 years old. Fortunately, her in-laws did not object to her being in school. They tentatively permitted her to continue attending school, although the arrangement was temporary.

Srirangam's husband, Raghavachar, could not pursue his collegiate studies due to personal and domestic constraints. He was, however, absolutely supportive of his wife's schooling. She was tutored by her father till the age of 13 years. Then, she went to live with her in-laws.

Early and repeated pregnancies and childbirth challenged Srirangam. At times, she had to opt for the privilege of home-schooling. She made sure that she could resume regular schooling to catch up with her studies and complete her academic requirements.

She was the recipient of a Gold Medal, when she completed her Lower Secondary in September 1892, for her outstanding performance.

Rai Bahadur was extremely sorry that his child had to be pushed into the institution of marriage, at such an early age. He was thankful that she was allowed by her in-laws to pursue her schooling. He invested all the care, love, and guidance that he could, to foster his child's growth. He had faith in her resilience against all odds.

He was ecstatic when she completed her Lower Secondary School, winning a Gold Medal, despite having to juggle caring for two young babies at home, at the tender age of 16!

Srirangam graduated with distinction from Maharani's Girls High School in 1896. When she was advised to continue her collegiate studies at Central College, Bangalore, her father provided all the support and encouragement that she needed.

Along with her husband, Raghavachar, he provided her with moral support, especially when her relatives lost touch with her, and boycotted her family, just because she had dared to continue her studies! She had defied established norms that dictated that young ladies should stay within the confines of their homes.

* * *

Young Srirangam grew up in Mysore, and enjoyed the benevolence of her *Appa* (father), Ambil N. Iyengar. She was constantly in an environment where her father's world revolved around education, especially the education of girls. She was personally tutored by him, among other deserving girls. The families of some of these girls happened to reach out to him, for advice or council.

Srirangam watched how zealously and passionately her father and his friend, M. Venkatakrishnaiah, worked together. She was astonished at what a neat team these two men had formed, being there for each other in their mission, and being there for young girls.

Srirangam looked up to the two men with awe, reverence, and sheer adoration. She constantly observed and listened to their conversations. She was impressed by their care and compassion for girls. She had found her heroes in the two gentlemen. The idea that she should someday follow in their footsteps crossed her mind. They strongly influenced Srirangam, and became her role models at that impressionable age.

Srirangam gradually developed a keen interest in and a better understanding of the world around her. She began to understand that the entire community that she belonged to happened to exist in a rather restrictive social environment. People seemed to be caught up in a variety of blind beliefs, orthodoxy, prejudices, customs and rituals. It suited their own antique beliefs and practices.

There was a point in her college years, that she became interested in Hindu mythology and started studying the characters in the Mahabharata.

Out of sheer appreciation for her father, she compared him to Bheeshma Pithamaha. She revered her father like Bheeshma Charya, who cared selflessly not only for his family, but all those who deserved his care.

To her, her father was as selfless as Bheeshma Pithamaha.

The Story of Ambil Narasimha Iyengar

A.N.I. was a trailblazer in various ways. I'm going to tell you the story of my great-grandfather because he too was an extraordinary human being. You will be thrilled, as I am, to know that he was considered to be the father of girls' education in Mysore.

Born in 1842, he came from humble beginnings. He was an orthodox Brahmin belonging to the Srivaishnava Iyengar family. He was born in Ambil, in Thanjavur District. He came up in life because of his great respect for education. He was a self-educated, self-made individual, with great awareness and forethought. He had progressive ideas, and a deep sense of commitment, honesty, and loyalty.

A.N.I. teamed up with Sri. Venkatakrishnaiah, a renowned journalist of Mysore, who was also a social reformer and strong optimist. Hence, their pursuits were sincere and far-reaching.

"A.N.I. may be aptly termed as the Father and great patron of Women's Education in Mysore," says K. Subba Rao, in his book *Revived Memories* (page 384).

Sri. A.N. I, and Sri. M. Venkatakrishnaiah proposed starting a school exclusively for girls and toiled hard propagating the cause of girls' education. They tried to arrange meetings with the learned class of Brahmins who seemed to be high-thinking, influential individuals. Their persistent efforts to earn the support of the elite were initially disappointing. However, committed to their shared mission, they continued their efforts. They continued approaching people, N.I. in person, and M. V. through his daily newspaper, *Thayi Nadu*, which he had just initiated.

At last, the concept of school for girls was propagated among the citizens of Mysore. N.I. succeeded in persuading the people of Mysore, discussing with them some issues and difficulties that needed to be overcome to establish a school for girls. He offered his residence and some financial support from his pocket.

Srirangam's father was a man of strong conviction, and he persevered in his mission to achieve his goal.

The Support Enjoyed By Ambilnarasimha Iyengar

Rai Bahadur Narasimha Iyengar's integrity, exemplary personality, and strength of character made him endearing to most noteworthy people in Mysore.

Because of his unwavering loyalty to the royal family, A.N.I. had earned their trust and confidence. The king and queen of Mysore had immense faith in his progressive ideas, his motives, forethought, and principles. Maharani Kempananjammanni had implicit faith in his progressive ideas, views and intentions. She was in favour of him establishing a school to educate girls.

Dewan Rangacharlu was in office and was extremely compassionate to the cause of women. He was indeed an advocate of women's education and their emancipation.

A.N.I. himself summarises the growth and development of women's education in the Premier State of Mysore. He stated that it was a rather sensitive and delicate subject because the issue was closely related to the social economy. It needed an understanding of the existing sentiments, practices and even prejudices of the community. In this context, Henry Cunningham is said to have quoted at the North Indian Association in London, "Female education could not be undertaken by the government, and thus should be undertaken by individuals. It must be done by the educated women." (Puttanna Chetty, Mysore p36-37).

The indomitable challenge for A.N.I. lay in involving the conservative classes in the Movement and securing their appreciation. The results achieved were applauded by people across India as a "grand solution to our great social problems."

N. Iyengar offered his residence as a venue to start the school and even contributed financially towards this end (K. Subba Rao, Modern Mysore).

Accordingly, a school was started in March 1881 with 28 girls, first in a temple within the palace premises (History of Maharani's College for Women, Mysore, updated by Gowri Sathya, on January 20, 2013). Although establishing the girls' school was the brainchild of A.N.I., he had the support of patrons in the royal family, Dewan Rangacharlu, Venkatakrishnaiah, Narayana Shasthri and the benevolence of Maharani Kempananjammanni.

Ambil Narasimha Iyengar paid for scholarships out of his pocket for girls from humble backgrounds to attend school regularly.

Initially, Maharani's School made very slow progress for want of lady teachers. By then, the Government made some contributions to administrative measures. Gradually the number of literate girls multiplied. Thanks to the large donations of Iyengar and his consistent crusade, the strength and attendance stabilised. Gradually the movement of women's education was mobilised, making the crusaders triumphant.

Mr. Shama Rao, in his book *Modern Mysore (1881-94)*, states the following: "In its years, women's education owed its progress to the zealous services of Rai Bahadur." A.N.I. used all the influence he had to propagate the education of women, not to speak of the large sums of money spent towards this cause from his purse.

When K Subba Rao questioned Rai Bahadur, he learned that the latter had spent over Rs 2 lakhs from his pocket to fund the education of girls, besides grants from the royal family. His passion for supporting girls' education made him win friends from across the country.

"Women who came to him with fatherless children and weeping eyes never went back empty handed. No father could have been kinder to his children, than this selfless soul to suffering humanity" (Revived Memories p385).

Narasimha Iyengar expressed in 1889 that the school had the honour of a host of distinguished visitors. Albert Edward Victor of Wales was very pleased with the progress that he witnessed and applauded it. It also had the honour of a visit by the Maharaja and Maharani of Baroda who expressed their delight at the success of the school.

Robert Lethbridge said, "Maharani's School, with its enhanced success, worthy of the Maharaja's care and interest, may be regarded as one of the jewels in his crown" (Puttanna Chetty, Mysore p36-37).

Diwan Rangacharlu and his wife visited the school in 1889 to examine its curriculum. They were so impressed by its advancement and smooth functioning that they admitted two of their daughters to the school.

A.N.I. and Sri M. Venkatakrishnaiah's Social Reforms

A.N.I., the Father of girls' education, was extremely compassionate to girls and young women. He was supposed to have generously paid for scholarships from his personal funds, so that students and widows could regularly attend school, to enable them to get trained as nurses, midwives and teachers!

A.N.I. and M.V. were social reformers who strove together to revolutionise the lives of women. N.I. was extremely committed to the cause of educating women and empowering them by improving their social status. He stated that Maharani's Girls College deserved recognition for its work towards educating widows of all ages (Puttanna Chetty).

Despite the general apathy of the educated classes regarding this social issue, N. Iyengar took the lead in Mysore to remedy the problem. At least Mysore was trying to uplift this unfortunate lot through its measures and policies.

Rai Bahadur was extremely compassionate and kind to all women, including widows, who in a conservative society, had to suffer unfair hardships and meaningless restrictions, taboos and social constraints.

One of his important goals was to strive to bring about social reforms, to better the lives of these women, and to confer freedom, empowerment, social status and privileges on them, on a par with men.

Coincidentally, the Head of the Sringeri Matt and His Holiness, the Parkala Matt Swamy (Head of the Srivaishnava Community), seemed to have expressed their favourable opinions in support of educating widows. As religious Heads of the Brahmin community, they found it ridiculous and unfair to confine widows to seclusion, restricting their lifestyle, and their attire, for no valid reason.

Narasimha Iyengar was highly influenced, motivated and impressed when he read about Dundo Keshav Karve, who had founded an educational institution for Hindu widows in Poona in 1906.

According to Rai Bahadur, Mysore had initiated the system of educating widow pupils, by awarding scholarships to widows in the schools and homes within the respective province. A home for widows was established in Mysore in 1907. There were other homes for widows started to help widowed pupils. These homes safely housed the out-of-station pupils. Ashrams were also proposed to enable quite a few widows to be trained as midwives, nurses and teachers.

One of my great grandfather's favourite, and often repeated saying was, "If India is ever to be saved, and it is ever to rise high in the scale of nations, it should be through the instrumentality, through the culture and devotion and enlightened sacrifices of our women in general, and of our widows, in particular. That is the most sacred task I am engaged in." (A.N.I. in K. Subba Rao's *Revived Memories*, p 385).

My great-grandfather spent the entire amount that had been saved and set aside by the family for a pilgrimage to Kaashi (sacred religious place), towards starting and establishing a widow's home in Mysore. I am filled with pride to share with you that this task was as sacred as Kaashi for him and his family.

Sri. M. Venkatakrishnaiah was indeed a social reformer. He was vigilant and did not miss any social anomaly that was prevalent in society towards the end of the 19th century.

He initiated discussions on the problem of *Nauch* girls, (the dancing girls, court dancers) who were being exploited by the affluent classes. They were patriarchal in their attitudes and had multiple standards related to modesty, morality, dignity, and respect for women. He had discussions with significant and influential members of the Literary Union and persuaded them to take a pledge, not to encourage dancing as a means of entertainment during marriages, and other public and private events.

He thereby put an end to the *Nauch* system and other related social evils, like prostitution. Such exploitation was prevalent and in vogue during the British Era, in Mysore.

Srirangam's Pursuits and Strides Were Far From a Bed of Roses

(1889-1892)

I want to share with you my grandmother's story so that you will better understand the sociocultural climate of the period. Srirangam's progress in education, her accomplishments, including that of winning a Gold Medal, and all the applause she received from her teachers and father did not happen on a bed of roses.

Srirangam was supposed to have sobbed bitterly at the thought of getting married and having to give up her education. At the tender age of 10 years, she was married to a young man from a rather orthodox background. While she attended Maharani's Girls School, she was still being tutored by her father till she was 13 years old. There was another big and daunting change in her life around this time. At the end of her 13th year, she endured a pregnancy and gave birth to a baby girl, who died as an infant! Srirangam had the misfortune of losing her firstborn child.

Her father regretted having pushed her into marriage as a child, despite his own progressive outlook. But he was also a victim of conservative and patriarchal practices of the period. He gave in to the social pressure of having to marry off his brilliant child. He was forced to adhere to the community's belief that a girl had to be married off as a child! Srirangam's own mother and grandmother were bent on this belief.

However, Iyengar found solace in the fact that Srirangam was allowed to pursue her schooling. He invested all the care, love and guidance necessary for her growth and progress. He was convinced of Srirangam's resilience against all odds. To his great delight and pride, she was awarded the Gold Medal in 1892 for her outstanding performance. Being a great patron of girl's education, Honourable Chentsal Rao attended the graduation at Maharani's School and presented the award to her.

Srirangam continued her education, as Maharani's Girls School emerged as a High School in 1893. She completed her High School with outstanding records in 1896.

Relocation of Srirangam's Family to Bangalore

(1896-1899)

Srirangam probably had to take a break to prepare to relocate to Bangalore with her young children, her elderly parents-in-law, and her mother. She was fortunate to have the unwavering support of her father, and her husband, Sri. Raghavachar. They helped her remain stable and grounded despite a host of challenges in a much bigger city, and under new circumstances.

The two important men in her life were by her side as she faced several challenges in the new environment. I'm glad to share with you her spirit of adventure. There were no means of public transport in Bangalore in those days. And the distance between her new residence in Chamarajapet and Central College, across Mysore Bank, was intimidating.

Accompanied by her maternal uncle's wife, Hiramoyi, she went to Lal Bhag Botanical Garden and practised bicycling. She then started cycling to Central College in her saree. Amba herself had told me how people would peep out of their windows, to look at the lady who had defied norms, not only to study further but to do so amidst men in an all-men's college!

My grandmother paved the way for herself to move forward, taking big strides despite challenges, and moving closer to her goal each step of the way.

* * *

I'm going to relate to you the incredible story of my grandmother who was the first woman graduate in the state of Mysore in 1903-06, more than a century ago. She was one among three girls to have completed their matriculation from Maharani's Girls High School. She was directed by Dewan Rangacharlu and the Royal Family of Mysore to pursue her collegiate education at Central College, Bangalore.

Sow. Rukmaniamma, who followed Srirangam, must have decided to wait until Maharani's Girls High School was upgraded to a second-grade college in 1902. Subsequently, she graduated from Maharani's College.

Srirangamma's curriculum consisted of Kannada and History as her core subjects. She had to pass one subject a year. Science, Geography, Maths and English had to be passed in the third year. She fell ill in her final year and had to retake her exam. She passed with a first class, ranking second, and graduated with a B.A. degree in 1903. She pursued her Honours course in English Literature and passed that as well.

My grandmother influenced many of her relatives, friends, and other young ladies to pursue their education. Srirangamma's cousin, Ammakuttiamma, followed her footsteps, among many other women who graduated from Mysore University. In 1908, Sow. Subbamma passed her Panditha Exam in Kannada on her very first attempt. Indiramma was the first woman to graduate in the *Okkaliga* Community (non-Brahmin) in 1924. She also received a Diploma in Education from Leads University, London, in 1928. (K.A. Gazetteer, p 654).

Even before the graduations were announced in1906 by Madras presidency, the Department of Education under British Rule absorbed both Srirangamma and K.D. Rukmaniamma. This was in recognition of the two ladies being educated, elite and emancipated young women, who could be assets to the Department, in terms of contributing to the quality of education in the state schools. Both of them were designated to the responsibilities of superintendents.

Rukmaniamma assumed office as the Superintendent, and Srirangamma as the Assistant Superintendent at Maharani's College, Mysore. She also started teaching English to college students, and was on a scale of Rs 200, grading to Rs 300. She was then deputed to teach in Bangalore. She was given an allowance and was provided a bungalow with three to four servants, including a cook. All of her students passed. Rukmaniamma taught an undergraduate class of three students, all of whom graduated successfully.

A.N.I. himself has summarised the growth and development of women's education in the princely state of Mysore. (Putanna Chetty…p34-43.) He had the foresight to ensure that women had to be educated! He recalled Sir Henry Cunningham's words at the National Indian Association, London: *Female Education could not be undertaken by the Government. Thus, it had to be undertaken by individuals. It had to be done by the educated women* (Putanna Chetty, p36-37).

The biggest challenge for A.N.I. and M. Venkatarishnaiah was to involve the conservative class in the movement to mobilise girls' education. Therefore, the leaders of this movement had to be cautious to avoid clashes. However, the results achieved were applauded by native gentlemen across India as "a grand solution to one of our great social problems." (Putanna Chetty, Mysore. P 44.)

Trials and Tribulations of the Two Crusaders to Stabilise the School

Sri. M. Venkatakrishnaiah enrolled his wife Parvathi in Maharani's Girls School, hoping to set an example for others to follow. Girls education however made very slow progress for want of women teachers.

Despite establishing the school and its management, the students were from poor Brahmin families. Rai Bahadur and N. Iyengar paid several parents an incentive for sending their daughters to school regularly. Thanks to the large donations made by N. Iyengar, and the strong support of the Maharaja and the Dewans, there was an increase in the number of students, and the attendance gradually stabilised. Gradually, the number of educated women multiplied.

N. Iyengar faced harsh criticism and vehement opposition from the community. Extremely vile rumours were spread about him. Ulterior motives were ascribed to the founder of the school. Eventually, the women's education movement was mobilised, to the absolute joy of the two crusaders. The Government of Mysore also joined the cause and made contributions through its administrative measures.

One day, K. Subba Rao questioned Rai Bahadur and learned that he had contributed over Rs 2 lacs from his personal earnings, besides the grants from the Royal Family. He generously gave scholarships to female students and widows for vocational training from his own pay and pension.

Thanks to Rai Bahadur's strict vigilance, the curriculum was periodically evaluated, to ensure that the standard of education was high. Changes were incorporated as deemed necessary.

It is interesting and intriguing to note that initially, the goal of educating women as per the expectations of the community, was something totally different. It was expected that such education would prepare young girls only for married life, rather than facilitating emancipation and empowerment!

A great deal of care was invested in ensuring their harmonious adjustment to married life. The educated girl was expected to be more aware of her role as a devoted and loving wife. She would also prepare to be a mother, who would be sensitive to the various needs of her children. In a nutshell, the school was deemed responsible for preparing a young girl for family life.

N. Iyengar was very particular indeed about the periodical evaluation of the school curriculum. He strove to add new and practical subjects and sought advice from the experts. He highlighted how the school tried to promote self-confidence in students, by introducing public speaking for the seniors (Puttanna Chetty). He also encouraged them to participate in extracurricular activities.

One of the outstanding features of M. G. High School in Mysore was the introduction of public speaking for senior students. One senior student ventured to deliver a lecture at Town Hall on Female Education in Mysore, which became a landmark speech in the history books. It is probable that as a senior student, Srirangam also participated in this activity.

A. N. I. himself spoke about his efforts to popularise women's education, which called for the serious attention of some leading members of the community in Mysore way back in the 1880s (Putanna Chetty, Mysore, p 36-37).

*Despite strong initial opposition, a resolution was passed that such a school had to be started with the aid of private donations. Only later, depending on its progress, government grants could be mobilised. Accordingly, a girls' school was started in 1881 with 28 students (History of Maharani's College for Women, Mysore, updated by Gowri Sathya, on Jan 20th 2013, p1).

Although establishing a girls' school in Mysore was the brainchild of Rai Bahadur, he had the immense support of its patrons in the Royal Family, Dewan Rangacharlu, Narayan Shasthri, and the benevolence of Maharani Kempananjammanni.

My great-grandfather proudly stated that in 1889, Maharani's Girls School had a host of distinguished visitors and boasts a record of their appreciation for the school. His Highness, Albert Edward Victor of Wales, visited the school. He was very pleased with its progress and he applauded it. The Maharaja and Maharani of Baroda, Gujarat, also visited the school. They expressed their delight at the school's high standards and success. Sir Robert Etheridge was another distinguished visitor who appreciated its success. He said it was worthy of the Maharaja's care and interest, stating it was "one of the jewels in the Maharaja's crown."

The institution was under the direct control of a lady superintendent since 1889 (Putanna Chetty Mysore, p 36-37).

Dewan Rangacharlu and his wife became suspicious of the school due to a misconstrued rumour and visited it in 1889 to examine the curriculum. They were so impressed with its smooth functioning that they admitted two of their daughters to the school. Eventually, the curriculum was further enhanced with the introduction of science subjects such as Chemistry and Physics.

Maharani's Girls School had a very impressive curriculum and the school imparted a high standard of education for girls, thanks to Rai Bahadur's periodical evaluations.

* * *

My great-grandfather was absolutely committed to the cause of women's education and their upliftment, and he left no stone unturned to succeed.

After Chamarajendra Wodeyar's ascension to the throne as the king of Mysore in 1881, N. Iyengar became the Maharaja's adviser, playing a major role in the king's court. Simultaneously, he established Maharani's Girls School.

It is said that once Ambil Narasimha Iyengar argued with the Maharaja, about the large amounts of money being spent on entertaining foreign dignitaries by hosting lavish banquettes. How could spending on women's education be considered a waste?

In the early decades of the 20th century, women's education gained momentum in Mysore state. Rai Bahadur was successful in diverting and utilising the prestigious Dev Bahadur Funds towards women's education. As a result, many young women were able to pursue their B.A. and M.A. exams (Bureau updated on Jan 18, 2018).

Women's education owed its progress to the zealous efforts of A.N.I. He not only used all the influence he had to educate women, but he also spent large sums of money on this noble cause (Shama Rao, Modern Mysore, P 685).

* * *

(1880-1881)

A.N.I. and M. Ventakrishnaiah initiated the proposal to start an exclusive school for girls and young ladies. At that time, the community in Mysore was not open to even the concept of girls leaving their homes to learn and become aware of the world outside!

Did you know that women in the Vedic period enjoyed equal status with men in all aspects of life? Verses in the Rig Veda suggest that women married at a mature age and were free to select their husbands. The Rig Vedas and Upanishads mention several female sages and seers like Gargi, Vachaknavi, and Maithreyi (7th Century BC).

In the Vedic Period, women had access to education and they could pursue any kind of learning, on a par with men. Over the years, they lost their status gradually, mainly because of disorientation and neglect. Eventually, the very idea of women's education in Mysore was seldom discussed and was put on the back burner and conveniently forgotten! The main reason behind this disproportionate and unfair misfortune is patriarchy.

The purdah system, the system of child marriages, the indifferent attitude of parents regarding the education of their daughters, and the general apathy of women when it came to asserting their rights, were major obstacles to the very idea of women's education. Accordingly, girls were forced to follow established customs and were confined to their domestic duties.

Their general appearance was the main criterion to assess whether they were eligible brides. Girls were good if they stayed at home, in rigid seclusion. This prevented them from having access to even elementary education. All this contributed to the general belief that only men were capable of learning and being educated.

Who do you think participated in propagating this theory? Girls across India remained uneducated, and continued being unaware of their deplorable state for centuries!

In the 1800s, there emerged many distinguished selfless people, who started thinking of this social anomaly and made efforts to start schools to educate girls. Among them were Jyothi Rao Phule, and his wife, Sow. Savithri Bai Phule, in Maharashtra, who started the very first school for girls in 1848.

Chandramukhi Basu, Kadambini Ganguly, and Anandi Bai Gopal Joshi were some of the earliest women to obtain a degree from Calcutta.

In the British Era, there was a revival of interest in women's education, although motivated by vested interests.

* * *

(1880)

Rai Bahadur and his friend's persistent efforts towards the betterment of young women are worth elaborating. This account throws light on how challenging their mission was. Both men invested a tremendous amount of care, hard work, persistence, and perseverance. They aimed to bring girls out of their confines so that they could be educated. The socio-cultural environment that they existed in was extremely restrictive.

The two pioneering crusaders of women's education, A.N.I. and M. Venkatakrishnaiah, continued their diligent and persistent efforts towards attracting the attention of the supposedly learned and enlightened men of the educated class. They arranged meetings with the seemingly high-thinking and influential individuals, to discuss the prospects of young girls and their emancipation through literacy and education.

What was the initial reaction and outcome of their efforts? The very thought of encouraging girls to leave their homes seemed outrageous to society! All their proposals fell on deaf ears. Some individuals vehemently disapproved and refused to support their cause. The very mention of a school for girls was treated as trivial!

The two reformers, however, persevered in their efforts to fulfil their mission with renewed vigour and conviction. But all their work towards this end was initially received with contempt and scorned at. It all appeared crazy to the invitees. They dismissed the matter with criticism. Some of them openly expressed mockery while others ridiculed Narasimha Iyengar.

How did my great-grandfather react? This kind of cold and rather negative response from the important members of the community only helped Narasimha Iyengar strengthen his resolve. It was evident to him how important it was to accomplish his goal.

The two partners reorganised themselves and got ready with their plan of action. They now worked with various new perspectives. Their experiences so far had sharpened their sensitivity. It helped them better understand the various circumstances that young women of the day may face. Therefore, they developed empathy for the predicament of women instead of merely pitying them.

So, the initial challenges and negative experiences of the two crusaders, in fact, enhanced their capability and fortified their commitment, to the cause of women! Hurray!

* * *

(1881-early-1900s)

The esteemed upper class in the 1800s believed that women didn't need to be independent or empowered at all, to any extent.

There were many prejudices held by Hindus. They felt that women didn't need to be employed and therefore they shouldn't be employed. Despite such extreme gender discrimination, women's education was not a priority. Women gradually started becoming aware, sought professional and vocational training and acquired employment, becoming independent and empowered, inspired by the work of Jyothi Rao and Savitri Bai Phule in Pune.

Dr. Ambedkar also focussed on women's education and empowerment. "I measure the progress of any community by the degree of progress women have achieved."

My great-grandfather elaborated on how a large number of women were being educated in Maharani's Girls College. Women's education had brought about a great revolution. It was in the interests of their social status. He also recognised and explained how much more hard work was necessary in this regard.

He acknowledged the support of His Highness, Maharaja Chamarajendra Wodeyar, and the interest of the Maharani Regent. He also acknowledged the support of the Royal Government and the cooperation of the many leaders of the orthodox sections of society and expressed his appreciation for such support.

Swamy Vivekananda said, "It is impossible to think of the welfare of the world unless the condition of women is improved."

His Highness, Chamarajendra Wodeyar himself said that women's education was essential for the wellbeing of the Hindu society.

Michele Obama said, "When girls are educated, their countries become stronger and more prosperous." (Praveen Kulkarni)

His Highness, the late Maharaja, at the ceremonial handing over of the new school building to M.G.H. School, said that he hoped it would continue to progress. According to him, it was the coincidence of opinions from people of various nations and religions, that provided an incentive for him to contribute to the progress of M.G.H. School, and to stabilise it.

* * *

Srirangamma's Personality

Do you know why I'm eager to share with you my Amba's story from August 1876 to February 1959? It's because of how empowered and emancipated she was more than a century ago. A retrospective overview of her entire incredible eventful life, in the light of the principles of gender equality and empowerment as laid down by state policy, showcases the quality of her life.

My amba was strong and stable under challenging circumstances. She was resilient during the difficult phases of her life during which she suffered grief and emotional upheavals. For a young lady, she was poised, maintained her dignity and composure, and had a strong personality. She was confident and adventurous, taking initiative to better her life. She was resourceful, took risks and learned new skills. She was equally adept at steering her own life even when she was in her eighties!

She had great self-awareness and empowered herself. She was discreet in planning for the future, to better the lives of women who needed an anchor, and steer social change. She challenged traditional restrictions and reservations, gaining freedom for herself, and encouraging other young spirited women to do the same.

It is worth noting that she single-handedly managed to shake off any limiting responses from members of her community. She didn't let the narrow attitudes of others, prejudices and subtle pressures thwart her own growth and progress in life. She fulfilled all her familial obligations, duties and responsibilities while working for the Department of Education. She made steady progress in promoting education.

She planned and acquired the composite property in Bangalore, and developed a part of it. She settled her daughters in marriage when they were much older than she was when she got married. She aptly educated her sons and got them married to educated grown women. Most importantly, she emerged as a matriarch of Kusum Bhavan, her abode of choice, amidst the richness of nature, without having to fight for her freedom!

Do you think that Srirangamma truly attained self-awareness and emancipation, and gave herself the gift of freedom, thereby enhancing the quality of her life?

* * *

My grandmother established a life of empowerment for herself and raised and educated her children. She also overcame the social pressures of a conservative community, the Srivaishnava Brahmins.

Remarkably, she did not succumb to the practice of child marriage when it came to her children. She had learned enough from her own experiences of being a *Balika Vadhu* at the tender age of 10 years. She had faced the challenges of early and frequent pregnancies, childbirth, and the death of her firstborn, while she was herself a child!

A) She made sure that her older daughter, Pankaja, was married when she was in her late teens, to Sri. Rangaswamy Iyengar. The couple settled down in Bombay, where the groom worked for a bank. They adopted their precious son, Doraiswamy, raised and educated him and got him married to a lovely bride, Jayalakshmi.

B) Her younger daughter, Kamala, was also married when she was in her late teens, to Sri. Rajagopala Chary, who worked in a high post at the Police Department in Tirunelveli District. They lived in South India and had five children.

My grandmother, as an educated lady, was not only self-aware but she had the courage to challenge the established social norms of those days, and lead a discreet life.

Srirangamma was discreet in acquiring brides for her sons and made sure that the girls had a minimum education of matriculation. Therefore, they were at least teenagers.

C) Her older son, Kitta, worked for the Mysore Electricity Board. He was married to a beautiful girl, Saroja, who was a prodigy in art. Saroja could draw exquisite portraits from her imagination, each of which was a masterpiece. She was also adept at drawing landscapes.

Srirangamma hired an art teacher for both her daughters-in-law and patronised the teacher's family. She appreciated and had great respect for art. She patronised talented individuals and displayed her daughter-in-law's artwork in her lavish drawing room and other parts of her house.

Kitta was talented in gymnastics and acrobatics. His mother arranged for him to get some lessons and training from a friend so that he could develop his talent.

Kitta and Saroja became parents to an extremely talented daughter, Vasantha, and a bright son, Narendra. Vasantha not only learned to sing Hindustani classical music, but she could also play the stringed instrument, Dilruba. She also learned Kathak from Pandith Govind Vittal and Laxmi Bhave and gave performances till she was married.

Kitta and Saroja's son, Narendra, took lessons at a flying school in Yelahanka, Bangalore, and learned to fly. He also enjoyed playing tennis and cricket.

Srirangamm's younger son, Sheshadri Raju, was married to Padma, also an educated young lady who was a teacher.

Srirangamma had respect for each family member's talent, encouraging and helping them develop and showcase their talents, and displaying their artwork in her house.

* * *

(1908-1926)

Srirangamma emerged as an emancipated and free woman, who attained gender equality and enjoyed a life of mutual respect, esteem, freedom and care in her personal relationships. She empowered herself with the liberty to make her own decisions.

In 1908, Raghavachar acquired a huge piece of land on 2nd Main Road, Laxmipuram, Mysore, measuring 148ft by 180ft. When Srirangamma was deputed to work in Mysore for 10 consecutive years, she and her husband personally supervised and built their home with a bank loan that she was able to procure. They lived in Vasantha Bhavan, surrounded by a garden, for almost 10 years.

With their hard-earned money and savings, Srirangamma and Raghavachar acquired a huge composite property in Malleswaram, Bangalore, in 1915. Eventually, they moved to Bangalore in 1916. They got a part of the property developed and built their home with personal supervision around 1925. It was large enough to house themselves and the families of their sons comfortably. They named it Kusum Bhavan (House of Fragrant Flowers). They planned to develop a garden filled with trees and flowers.

Amba and my grandfather lived happily with their two sons and their families. Two years went by in this abode of comfort, peace and tranquillity.

Does this account suggest that Srirangamma and her husband systematically planned and built their homes to ensure their comfort and future?

* * *

Sri Raghavachar took ill in 1926. Srirangamma had to face the challenge of taking care of him, making sure that he got the best medical care and supervision. She had to take prolonged leave, as she could not balance the two huge tasks, that of her work obligations, and caring for her husband. The entire family concentrated on grandfather's care and treatment.

In early 1927, my grandfather's health became worse. Grandmother organised the care of the head of the family, who was confined to bed. His diet and nutritional needs were entrusted to his older daughter-in-law, Saroja. Sow Padma was in charge of administering his medicines and maintaining his routine. Their two sons, Kitta and Raju, were in touch with the doctors and arranged for periodic visits. Grandmother herself stayed at his bedside and personally supervised the other members of the family.

The youngest member of the family was Vasantha, who was around 2 years old at that time. She constantly entertained and amused my grandfather by singing, dancing, playing around, and jabbering!

Even though the entire family rallied around him with utmost care and caution, Raghavachar passed away in the latter half of 1927. Srirangamma was shocked and grieved the loss of a very supportive and dear partner in life. It was a great personal loss. Her attempts to resume work failed. She had to opt for extended leave to heal and recover.

* * *

Srirangamma got promoted to Special Assistant to the DPI, despite her prolonged leave of absence.

(1931-onwards).

Srirangamma had varied interests and was involved in several activities after she retired from the Department of Education in 1931. She maintained her interest in literary activities. She invited young talented individuals periodically to her home, to discuss and share their talents as a means of mutual encouragement. She also participated in the welfare activities of Seva Sadan (orphanage and home for the destitute), and Mahila Samaj, (a women's association). She remained physically strong, active, and poised.

Despite challenges in her personal life, she remained balanced, mature, and mentally alert to manage her life with fortitude. She fulfilled the prophecy of her father, who had not underestimated her multi-tasking capabilities. I'm proud to share her approach of involving herself in constructive activities, to deal with her loneliness and grief.

(1927-onwards).

After 1927, her immense grief over the loss of her precious partner in life made her focus on improving the lives of destitute women, initially with literacy. She taught them to read the newspaper to increase their awareness about the world. She taught them to sign their names. With enhanced awareness, she became the Matriarch of Kusum Bhavan and managed the families of her sons, and grandchildren.

As a true emancipated, empowered woman, she created a refuge for destitute women and widows in her outhouse. There was a row of rooms in the northern part of her property that she converted into living quarters for just a token rent of Rs 10 per room. She also conducted regular evening classes to help them become literate, and eventually become teachers.

There were around eight to nine women, most of whom had one or two school-going children. The mothers were wage earners during the day and attended classes in the evening. Eventually, they all made progress. They became teachers or assistants in schools for young children. They educated their children as well.

One daughter became a Hindi Pandit and was employed as a teacher in the City Corporation High School. Her brother became a research scholar at the Indian Institute of Science, and eventually, went abroad for further research.

Do you think Srirangamma's intense sadness over losing an invaluable partner was sublimated to empowering women and their families through education? She made a positive impact on so many lives!

* * *

Srirangamma was indeed an educated individual who utilised the awareness that she had gained to take control of her personal and professional life. She was poised, independent, and modern. She challenged traditional constraints and empowered herself. Many young girls and women were inspired by her accomplishments.

Srirangamma became confident and adventurous enough to take initiatives to better her own life. She was resourceful and took risks to learn new skills so that she could steer her own life even when she was in her eighties! She methodically planned her life with awareness.

Srirangamma strove to better the lives of other women who needed support and steered a social movement to bring about change. Because she was readily accessible to solve their problems, she was popularly known as *Akkayya* (revered big sister/*didi*). She dedicated her life to creating a subtle uplifting change in society with her continuous efforts. Young women evolved from the confines of their dark attics. She was fondly addressed as 'teacher', as she helped everyone learn. She won the respect, love and trust of those who valued her guidance and the education she imparted.

* * *

My Amba's life rotated around education and awareness. She derived her own value system and stood by her convictions and principles. She tried to instil those values in the younger members of her family. She felt proud and happy whenever the youngsters of the family showed signs of strength of character. She believed they had developed these attributes from their education and by being self-aware.

She felt sad and disappointed when the young members of her family failed to imbibe the values she considered important, and assert their rightful privilege and empower themselves. She felt sad when they were tolerant of deprivation, gender discrimination, and abusive patriarchal dominance at home. All these unflattering attributes and subservience, despite their education and self-awareness, were heart-wrenching for her.

Amba was fully aware that every individual had to strive hard, earn and give certain gifts to themselves, thereby commanding a certain sense of self-worth. Do you realise that however sincere and fervent the intentions may be, no one can spoon-feed or inject these precious values into you? Mere literacy or even a university degree alone, does not guarantee all the fringe benefits of true education, of actual awareness and empowerment.

Amba strove relentlessly to bring about social change and a revolution in the attitude of girls and young women at every available opportunity, to enable social and economic order in the lives of young ladies.

* * *

(1935-1940)

Amba's own positive outlook and attitude impacted her entire family, and those who interacted with her. She typically asserted her right to freedom of judgement. She did not let the attitudes of the people in her community limit her views and actions.

She was surrounded by a community of people with conservative ideas and established practices. Despite creating awareness, over time, the archaic way of thinking and attitudes towards women continued to be subtly oppressive and were normalised.

Amba did not let this narrowmindedness thwart her own growth, or that of the women in her family. In fact, she did not even tolerate her own son treating his wife with contempt and being abusive. She approached him immediately. She first acknowledged how broadminded and compassionate he usually was towards girls and women. She appreciated him for his gentleness, but questioned his dual standards when it came to his own wife. She surprised him by grabbing his wrist, looking into his eyes, and speaking to him sternly. She reminded him that, "Charity begins at home." As a mother, she reinforced his big-hearted values, while she absolutely denounced his deplorable treatment of his own gentle and beautiful wife at home. She made it loud and clear that she fully supported her daughters-in-law, and had zero tolerance for such behaviour by any of the men in her family.

Hurray for Amba! Hurray for women's empowerment!

(Late 1930s)

In another family crisis, she had to denounce the neglect and abuse of women. To her utter shock, she found out that her younger son-in-law was polygamous, and had children from each marriage! Though she herself was a grieving widow and had just retired, she refused to sit around feeling helpless. She was gutsy enough to rush to Tirunelveli (Tamil Nadu, South India).

Srirangamma made an immediate trip to South India, and announced that she had to speak to the gentleman. She truly believed that all women should have freedom and be respected. She was an emancipated lady herself. She spoke to him sternly in the privacy of his residence, without having to be disrespectful. However, she realised that she was clueless as to how she could remedy the situation. She did her part and advised the gentleman, to ensure that his wife and five children would not become victims of neglect or abuse.

However, a short while after, her son-in-law suddenly died due to a heart ailment. Srirangamma rushed again to embrace the entire family and rescued them from hardship and lack of support. Her daughter's family was immediately relocated, and housed in Kusum Bhavan. Her residence could of course accommodate everyone. Suddenly, her family had doubled in size!

As head of the family, she called all the members of the household and spoke to them. She elaborated and explained the true meaning of family in terms of caring for one another's needs. She announced and supported every member of her extended family. She taught them to wait for their turn, to be tolerant, to share, and to adjust themselves within the joint family.

She managed the four adults, the four children of her two sons, in addition to her daughter and her five children remarkably well. With typical forethought, she began planning to house her daughter with self-respect, and self-sufficiency. She intended to gift the house to her daughter's oldest son, who, by then, had shown signs of taking initiative and responsibilities.

Srirangamma was indeed a brave lady who did not shirk in her efforts to stabilise the lives of her daughter and her five children. Once again, she stood her ground, respected each family member, cared for their needs, and fostered self-respect, self-sufficiency and independence.

(Early 1940s)

Srirangamma was truly pragmatic and was a person of fore-thought. She carefully constructed the independence of her younger daughter's children. She also wanted to foster self-sufficiency and self-reliance among the growing children. Thus, she procured a housing loan from Co-op Bank, with the plan to build a house in the adjacent plot next to her residence. She personally supervised the construction in the early 1940s.

Meanwhile, her daughter's oldest son completed his college degree and showed promise by taking initiative to join an Army school. Amba was discreet and perceptive of the young man's progress. She made a gift deed, leaving the house to her favourite grandson. Eventually, to her great satisfaction, she observed her grandson become independent, advance in his career, and assume responsibility for his mother and siblings.

Srirangamma helped her oldest granddaughter get married and settle down. The rest of the children were encouraged to continue their schooling. She was ecstatic when the youngest of her granddaughters followed in her footsteps, graduating with a B.A. Honours in English Literature.

Srirangamma recognised the talent in her young granddaughter, Malathi, and arranged Hindusthani classical music lessons for her under the tutelage of the resident music teachers, Pandith Govind Vitthal and Laxmi Bhave. Her older granddaughter, Vasantha, also attended the music lessons. Malathi learned to sing melodiously and continued taking music lessons till her graduation from college. Srirangamma proudly enjoyed her granddaughter's singing.

Do you think Srirangamma's mission of settling her daughter's family was accomplished? Did she provide everyone a chance to develop their strengths and talents, enabling them to become self-reliant?

* * *

I wish to elaborate on my Amba's outstanding attitude towards life. She typically stood by her convictions and seldom let anyone infringe on the self-respect and reverence she commanded. She was truly a gentle lady who quietly wielded a life of great respect and dignity.

These were indeed remarkable attributes which my Amba emulated within her immediate surroundings. She did not let her conservative or orthodox family background or any circumstance limit her growth.

Even at work, with the Department of Education, Srirangamma commanded respect from both her colleagues and subordinates alike. She was extremely committed to her work, took pride in her progress, and discharged her official obligations with diligence. She was also highly principled.

Her calibre of work as an Assistant to the D. P. I. was highly professional. She took the initiative to be on the Board of Text Book Committees, and regularly engaged in pursuits to improve and enhance educational facilities. She was in constant touch with the AIWC and worked with Mrs Thackeray and others. She utilised her freedom fully to exercise her choice to contribute towards honorary work towards women's upliftment. These activities kept her busy, serene and satisfied, but not for too long. Abrupt and rude interruptions typically came from the home front!

Being a woman of immense fortitude and maturity, how do you think she faced life? She took things in her stride, continuing her eventful journey with remarkable balance and stability.

* * *

(1940s)

As mentioned before, Srirangamma was born into a rather orthodox family but was fortunate to be raised in an environment of enlightenment. She grew up to be broadminded in her outlook and thinking. A good education paved the way for her positive attitude and open-mindedness, where she was free of biases. These attributes were also the result of her own maturity and awareness.

Srirangamma's own *Maama* (maternal uncle), Dr. Ramaswamy Iyengar, returned to Bangalore, after specialising in Ophthalmic Surgery in London in 1907. He established the famous Minto Hospital in Bangalore city. He happened to marry an educated Bengali woman from Calcutta.

Soon after, Srirangamma's favourite maternal cousin brother, Seshadri Iyengar, an Electrical Engineer, returned from Columbia University in 1907. He happened to marry the younger sister of the Bengali woman, Prabha. In an era when inter-community marriages were unthinkable, accepting such circumstances would generally be a culture shock, especially for Srivaishnava Iyengars.

However, it is worth acknowledging and appreciating Srirangamma's views on this matter. She had no reservations about accepting her uncle's and cousin's inter-cultural marriages to the young ladies, by their choice. She related to and freely mixed with the two new Bengali relatives and their children. In fact, Hironmayi (Hirnmoyi is the Bengali pronunciation) became Srirangamma's best friend, and they both learned to bicycle together at the Lalbagh Botanical Gardens.

Srirangamma even travelled to Calcutta and Lucknow in 1940, to participate in her nephew, Amar Iyengar's wedding, and enjoyed the hospitality offered by her relatives. She also invited her relatives and reciprocated their hospitality at home, in Bangalore.

She was extremely fond of her two nieces, Seshadri's daughters, Ramola and Kunthala. She periodically entertained them at Kusum Bhavan, her home in Malleswaram. She also visited them both in their residences in Richmond town, as long as she lived.

She made extra efforts to be in touch with her favourite niece, Ramola Chatterjee. She even contacted the latter when she visited Bombay, at the tail end of her life, and visited her home in Colaba in August 1958.

Isn't it remarkable that she could free herself of biases, and get along with her Bengali relatives without any reservations?

It is interesting to note that Srirangamma, her *Maama*, Ramaswamy Iyengar, and cousin brother, Seshadri Iyengar, all grew up in the same household, that of their grandmother Laxmi. Each one of them seemed to hail from a family of trailblazers who were talented in various ways.

Dr. Ramaswamy established the Minto Hospital and strove his whole life to help the visually impaired. Seshadri Iyengar helped to establish Asia's First hydroelectric plant in Shvana Samudram Falls. He first generated electricity in Kolar Gold Fields and then brought electric light to Bangalore. Srirangamma propagated education and awareness among the people of Mysore state. Each one of them brought different kinds of luminance thus impacting the lives of people.

* * *

Srirangamma's younger son, Sheshadri (Raju), graduated in law and initially started working in Bombay. Eventually, he moved to Bangalore. His mother supported his choice to marry a lovely well-educated girl, Padma, who was a science teacher in a high school. Padma's parents were Amba's younger brother, Anujan Varadhan, and Chechi, both of whom succumbed to influenza in their youth. Srirangamma chose to raise and educate Padma. Padma's older sister, Jaya, was raised and educated by Srirangamma's younger sister, Alamelamma, in Mysore.

Sheshadri and Padma loved each other and were happily married. They had a girl, Vijaya, who grew up to be very bright, and when she was 4 years old, they had their second child, Sujaya (me).

In April 1942, Sheshadri started facing health issues and was placed under medical treatment. After a few months, he went to stay with his brother's family in Bhadravathi, where his favourite sister-in-law Saroja took excellent care of his dietary requirements and routine. Since his condition deteriorated, he returned to Bangalore, where his mother and family made sure that he received the best care. His wife, Padma, quit her teaching job and concentrated on caring for him. However, his health became worse and towards the end of that year, he passed away, to the utter grief of his mother, wife, and the rest of his family.

Srirangamma lost interest and the zest to run the Montessori school that she had established on her property. Thus, she closed it. She had to take care of Padma and her young child. She was gripped with absolute sadness and despair.

Kitta and his family moved back to Bangalore to be supportive of Srirangamma and his sister-in-law.

The romantic marriage between Sheshadri and Padma was so short-lived, abruptly being cut short by death.

Challenges Srirangamma Faced in Pursuing Her Education

I have already shared with you Srirangamma's story and what an incredible celebrity she had become in the early 1900s. However, it was not all glory and celebrations. It must be acknowledged that she was not spared the tremendous challenges that came with being educated.

My Amba faced many of the same problems that girls face even today, both in suburban and rural India, to attend school regularly. Amba belonged to the generation that was subjected to, and overshadowed by patriarchal practices. This meant that the male folk and society as a whole believed that men were far superior than women. They believed that girls belonged within the four walls of their home. Women did not need to attend school to acquire an education, to learn, or to be liberated from their domestic chores!

Amba was indeed a victim of child marriage, as she was married when she was just 10 years old. She was subjected to recurrent pregnancies and childbirth! It was very unfortunate that as a child herself, she had to endure the death of her firstborn child. She had to do household chores too, apart from caring for her two infants, around the time she was awarded the gold medal in 1892, for being a pioneering candidate and completing her lower secondary education with distinction.

She took advantage of the then-available alternative of home schooling. She was taught at home by teachers who came home. She made sure that the break from regular school was only a stop-gap arrangement to cope with the pregnancies and childbirth. She had to contend with a newborn infant and two toddlers, as she was clearing her high school requirements and examinations. She worked hard to make up for lessons missed and caught up with the required standard of studies.

Amba was well aware of the tremendous support of her husband. She was fully appreciative of how very fortunate she was. She was indeed aware of how her in-laws and husband, Sri Raghavachar, were not gripped by patriarchal shackles, and were indeed generous, despite being part of the orthodox community.

My grandfather's extraordinary maturity in not viewing his wife's progress as a threat to him, was truly admirable. He must have been a trailblazer of that generation. The outstanding support of Srirangamma's in-laws, which was applaudable, helped her accept her circumstances as the norm, and she did not resent her predicament or wallow in self-pity. Her father, A.N.I., was amazingly free of patriarchal influences and was adequately supportive of Srirangamma's progress.

Because of her own positive attitude, Srirangamma was able to pursue her graduation, as she was a go-getter. It is interesting to note that she conceived her fourth child during her college years, giving birth in her senior year of undergraduate studies in 1901.

Srirangamma seems to have had incredible motivation and tenacity to pursue her education. When there was no public transportation in Bangalore city, the enormous distance between her home and college did not intimidate her. She simply became resourceful and practised bicycling. She cycled from Chamarajapet to Central College, in Mysore Bank Circle, Majestic, on her own!

What might seem puzzling to us was how she managed to cycle in her nine yard saree worn in the *Madisharu* (Iyengar) style! Is it not evident that my Amba held on to any anchor that was accessible, and marched on with determination towards her ultimate goal? Do you think that she may have been a quiet rebel, bent on reaching her objectives at any cost?

What is remarkable is that Srirangamma very much remained in the system, conformed to the existing norms to a certain extent, fulfilled most of the standard obligations, and simultaneously followed her own path. She had no need to run away, rebel and alienate herself to pursue her goal!

* * *

Anecdotes Related to
Srirangamma's Career

January 16, 1901-1931

Both Srirangamma and K.D. Rukmaniamma were consumed by their responsibilities at the Department of Education. They were emancipated ladies who were considered assets, in terms of enhancing and contributing to women's education. Both of them started their career with the Department in Maharani's College, Mysore.

Rukmaniamma started off as the Assistant Mistress of the College. Srirangamma too started as the Assistant Mistress in Maharani's College. She taught English and the vernacular to the senior students. She was the senior most teacher. She also compered many of the events in school and was in charge of managing such functions throughout the year.

On July 10, 1916, Srirangamma was posted as the Head Mistress of Vani Vilas Institute, in Bangalore. There, she initiated short-term and long-term planning for the Institute. She was already involved in teaching the senior most class, besides supervising the performance of the entire staff. She provided guidance to junior teachers and parents. She handled the highest responsibility, that of managing the school, and provided regular feedback to higher authorities.

As an Inspector of Schools, in Bangalore, she was appointed to assess the instructional standards of schools and determine whether the education rendered by the respective schools was satisfactory. She held the most responsible post in the management and supervised the schools and their respective staff members.

The purpose of this book is to narrate the incredible story of my dear paternal grandmother, who raised me from infancy. Srirangamma challenged traditional restrictions and attained self-empowerment, influencing and inspiring other young ladies in Mysore state to do the same. She worked to attain gender equality for herself and raised and educated her children.

The Department of Education certainly considered the pioneering lady graduates as great assets. The fresh graduates were absorbed into the Department, which was under British rule then, as educated and poised young ladies could certainly contribute to education in general, and to the education of women in particular.

Srirangamma and K. D. Rukmaniamma were both employed in early 1901, even before they had completed their graduation. Till then, there were no Hindu women employed in the Government Departments. Srirangamma took on the post of Assistant Mistress in Maharani's College on January 16, 1901. She started teaching English and the vernacular. Smt. K.D. Rukmaniamma also assumed the post of Assistant Mistress on February 1, 1901. She taught English and Kannada. A few other Indian women were also employed after they graduated.

Srirangamma continued in this post till July 1, 1906, when she was promoted as Assistant Mistress (civil list # 1915). On July 10, 1914, she became Assistant Superintendent in Maharani's College (ref, Quarterly Civil List #2, up to Jan 1, 1915). She assisted in supervising and managing the staff. She worked well with the school leaders to satisfy the needs of the students, and to meet district goals. She worked diligently and was responsible for keeping the Board of Education informed of the events and happenings in the district. She worked briefly in this post, as she was posted as the Headmistress of the Girls High School on July 1, 1915 (Civil list #3, 1916).

As Headmistress, Srirangamma was the senior-most teacher in Bangalore and was involved in instructing the senior-most class. She led the school's happenings and managed its functioning throughout the academic year (Civil list #4, 1916).

On July 10, 1916, she was posted as the Headmistress of Vani Vilas Institute, Bangalore. There, she was responsible for short-term and long-term planning as regards the functioning of the Institute. She was actively involved in teaching the senior most class, besides supervising the entire staff (Civil list #5, 1919). She provided guidance to the junior teachers, in-service staff, assistants, and parents. She also provided periodical feedback to the higher authorities.

While Srirangamma was still the Headmistress of Vani Vilas Institute, she was posted as Inspector Of Department (IOD) of the girls' schools, Bangalore (Civil list #6, 1924). Her responsibilities included examining the schools to determine whether the standard of education rendered by them was satisfactory (Civil list #6, 1924).

As Headmistress, she was responsible for managing the school and its staff members. She planned the activities of each class, its strengths, and goals. She organised the grades, deciding on the number of sections, the class size, the adult-to-child ratio, and the number of assistants available to teachers.

Srirangamma taught English, prose and poetry to the senior classes. She provided guidance to the teachers through feedback, periodic counselling, and planned weekend workshops. She voluntarily enrolled herself to be a Board Member of the Textbook Committee, so that she could contribute to improving the standard of the instructional material.

Between 1923 and 1926, she was appointed alternatively as Inspector of Schools and Headmistress of Vani Vilas Institute, because she was very good at both roles.

1931 – Eat Shamelessly

Srirangamma was inspector of schools when she was invited for lunch along with all the primary school teachers, in her honour. The host was a North Indian who spoke Hinglish with a strong accent. As the host served the food, she said, "Madam, please eat shamelessly," in an attempt to be hospitable.

The quick-witted Srirangamma retorted, "Please do not worry, I am all fed up!"

* * *

She was resourceful and learned to drive a car. She drove her T Ford Hatchback to rural schools and far-off urban schools, escorted by a young teenager. He was also trained to cook for her, especially when she had to stay overnight.

* * *

Another humorous Hinglish anecdote – Don't embrace me.

A North Indian Head Master introduced Srirangamma to his teachers, and said, "Teachers, make sure your documents are all organised for Madam to inspect."

"Please do not embrace (embarrass) me," he continued.

The teachers reassured him with a chuckle saying, "We will never embrace you, Sir!"

"Hot snakes (snacks) will be served with tea."

That sounds so appetising, Sir."

* * *

In 1923, Srirangamma was posted as Inspector of Schools once again. Between 1923 and 1925, she worked as Inspector of Schools in Mysore (Civil list #8,1927).

In 1926, Raghavachar became ill. Srirangamma had to face the challenge of taking care of him at home. She made sure that her husband got the best medical care that was available at that time. She assigned duties to every member of the family as regards his care and attention. She supervised his care and stayed at his bedside.

She tried resuming her work, but she could not give her best as she was too anxious and distracted. When he passed away in 1927, the sudden loss of a very supportive partner was a tremendous shock and setback. Although she was grief-stricken, she tried to gradually resume work. But, she had to take prolonged leave again, to allow herself the time and space to heal.

Despite her long leave of absence, she was promoted to the post of Lady Assistant to the D.P.I., on 1.11.1927 (Civil list #9, 1929). She assisted the Director in his daily agenda. She requested that she be familiarised with the different responsibilities that she was expected to handle in the new role. She procured the necessary instructions from the Director regarding the meetings to be attended in coordination with the concerned officers.

She arranged tours and meetings headed by the Director and accompanied him on such tours. She also maintained the minutes of the meetings. She took the initiative and responsibility to coordinate with public representatives, teachers and the general public when they visited the Director at his office. She was appreciated for her excellent Public Relations skills.

* * *

Srirangamma continued her role as the Special Personal Assistant to the D.P.I., by executing the duties related to the personal section of the Director. She assisted the Director in implementing the major plans and programmes of the Department within the stipulated time frame. She promptly consulted and clarified the Director's instructions from time to time. She gradually earned the trust and confidence of the Director with regard to her efficiency and diligence. She corresponded with various officers to collect information with regard to legislative sessions or legislative committees and passed on the information to the Director.

Srirangamma continued to be empowered. She was indeed a gentle lady who quietly wielded a life of great respect and dignity. This was indeed a remarkable attribute, given her circumstances. She did not let her conservative background, or any other circumstances, intimidate or thwart her growth. Even at work, at the Department of Education, she commanded the respect of her colleagues and subordinates. She established gender equality and worked well with all her colleagues.

She was extremely committed to her work, took pride in it and discharged her official obligations with diligence. Her calibre of work as Special

Assistant to the D.P.I. was professional (Civil List #11, 1910 and Civil List #12, 1930). She took initiative and regularly engaged herself in pursuits to enhance the education facilities.

In 1931, Srirangamma retired from the Department of Education. She performed all her duties as a Special Personal Assistant to the D.P.I. to the best of her abilities, earning the appreciation of her superiors and colleagues. She contributed to the success of the Department by simultaneously working as the Inspector of Schools. Therefore, she enjoyed the praise and recognition for her courageous work (Civil List #10, 1929).

* * *

Srirangamma had varied interests and was engaged in several activities after her retirement from the Department in 1931. To showcase her positive attitude and balance in life, I must talk about how she participated in constructive activities.

Srirangamma was interested in literary activities. She invited young talented people to her home periodically, to have discussions and share their talents. "Her home was like a Parisian salon, a hub of intellectual discussions, where distinguished thinkers, budding writers, musicians and artists used to meet," as Pandith Rajeev Taranath told her nephew, Professor M.N. Panini.

She also regularly participated in the welfare activities of Sthree Samaja, Seva Sadna, (orphanage and home for the destitute), and Mahila Samaja. She remained physically strong and carried herself with poise.

Despite challenges in her personal life, she maintained her composure and was mature and mentally alert. She fulfilled the prophecy of her father, Ambil Narasimha Iyengar, who had not underestimated her strength in multi-tasking.

* * *

Srirangamma was also a role model and source of inspiration. She had a positive influence on innumerable young ladies. Soon after her graduation, a few schoolmates, and relatives, including her cousin Ammakuttiamma, followed in her footsteps and pursued their collegiate education.

Srirangamma's juniors like Smt. Subbamma, Nagamma, and Vengadamma managed to complete their graduation. Most of them also started working for the Department of Education, becoming educators. She was able to mobilise a socio-cultural movement, resulting in the empowerment of women, and the upliftment of their socio-economic status.

Srirangamma, as a Head Mistress of Vani Vilas Institute, is said to have gone door to door in Bangalore, like a social worker would, persuading parents to send their daughters to school. Sometimes, people shut their doors on her face, and said that they did not want their daughters to become like Srirangamma! They feared that their girls may not be eligible for marriage, and may remain social boycotts.

Srirangamma did not give up but pursued her sincere efforts to get girls out of their homes and go to school. On subsequent visits, she encouraged families to send their teen widows to school, so that they could have a life of their own, instead of living couped up in attics and basements! Eventually, she was successful in gathering a group of girls who were admitted to Vani Vilas Institute, where they completed their high school education.

She started teacher training programmes, because there was a dearth of girls' schools, due to a shortage of female teachers.

Later, she provided a refuge for young destitute women, housing them in a part of her own property. She taught them how to read and write. They learned how to sign their names and read the newspaper. She tutored them to complete matriculation as private candidates. Most of them became teachers or assistants in schools for young children. These economically empowered ladies in turn educated their own children!

In one teacher's family, the daughter became a teacher. The oldest son studied Law. The second son became a research scholar and a professor in the US. Two more sons became accomplished engineers!

* * *

Srirangamma was well aware that she was extremely fortunate to have a soulmate who was truly respectful and supportive of her educational and professional pursuits. However, she was also well aware of the societal constraints, and the patriarchal attitudes that women had to face. She was well aware of the biases against women, and the subtle domination and oppression they suffered.

She never assumed that mere education and employment alone would ensure the empowerment of women. It was crucial that women were aware of their own rights, and assert the same, to command fairness, respect, and consideration in their personal and professional life.

Srirangamma frequently told women, "You must assert your right to freedom, and give yourselves the gift of self-respect. You should not become the sacrificial goat. Each of you is an educated individual who is aware that it is your right to think, decide, choose and participate in life."

"Ideally, you may have the patience and forbearance of Mother Earth, but you need to invoke the Durga (the aggressive form of Mother) in you, to ensure that justice and fairness prevail, without having to be antagonistic."

Grandmother often spoke to all the young ladies, and the children of her family, including me and Geeta, who were growing up under her influence. Srirangamma appreciated and rejoiced to see the girls in her family blossom into young ladies with the fortitude, awareness and grit to empower themselves.

It was heart-wrenching for her when any family member succumbed to patriarchal obsessive domination! Two of Srirangamma's granddaughters and great-granddaughters turned out to be fortunate enough to enjoy lives of gender equality, mutual respect, and understanding in their personal lives.

Her only grandson, Narendra, who was raised under her influence, grew up to be absolutely gentle. He turned out to be a thorough gentleman, sensitive to the views of others, and exemplified fairness, kindness and absolute respect for women.

One of Srirangamma's granddaughters, and two of her fourth-generation female descendants, completed their post-graduation in English literature. One of her granddaughters specialised in Early Childhood Development and Early Education. Of the four, three of them chose to be educators.

In my childhood, I had dreamed of starting a school, and was blessed when that dream came true. I founded the lovely preschool Kreedangan (play quadrangle), on a part of Srirangamma's property in October 1981.

* * *

I was extremely fortunate to have the moral support, help and encouragement of my extended family and friends, in establishing and developing the preschool.

One of Srirangamma's great-granddaughters completed her M.Phil in Sociology, while another worked in the Indian Civil Service. One of Srirangamma's female descendants (fourth generation) and another from the fifth generation asserted their right to dignity and freedom, and have succeeded in empowering themselves.

Another fourth-generation descendant has ensured a life of absolute empowerment for herself. She enjoyed the freedom to achieve whatever she wanted. She studied and worked in Science, Engineering, and Environmental Law.

Thanks to my great grandmother's blessings, Ms Geeta Sunderrraj earned several degrees to her credit and specialised in Education. She worked as an educator in several countries, and eventually served as the Head of Seoul International School, Korea, for several years. Her achievements were indeed commendable! Geeta grew up with me under my grandmother's influence. We shared a childhood full of fun and mutual care. She was an empowered woman who led an independent life. While serving as an educator, she raised and educated two brilliant daughters.

At least six women of Srirangamma's fifth-generation descendants have all known nothing but self-empowerment, freedom and independence. This could probably be because of their being adequately educated, their awareness, and their exposure to global interactions.

Two of the young ladies, Ms. Sridevi and Ms. Supriya, are empowered women who have earned gender equality, mutual respect and freedom in their personal lives. Professionally, both of them are brilliantly accomplished attorneys of good standing. Before working as a Corporate lawyer, Geeta's daughter Supriya, was a local and state prosecutor.

Two young ladies of the fifth generation are accomplished and brilliant engineers who are also empowered and enjoy gender equality. Another fifth-generation descendant, Audrey, is currently pursuing her Ph.D in Public Policy. She works on policy research related to women's empowerment and preventing gender-based violence. Audrey's sister is also working on her Doctorate in a similar field.

A century ago, Srirangamma strove to expose women to education in Mysore state, helping them become teachers to better their lives and status.

Do you readers agree with me that Srirangamma would find it highly gratifying to acknowledge the accomplishments and empowerment of her descendants?

* * *

My extraordinary grandmother, Srirangamma's life was full of dynamic changes, incredible challenges and adventure. Thus, her life was highly eventful. Do you know why her story is so special? It is because she was an incredible trailblazer who defied ancient norms. She dared to challenge established social restrictions, and mobilised change.

Srirangamma was Amba to me. She was my childhood hero, who became my Guru, my fond friend and patron. This story is about each of the ordinary days we spent together, starting from when I was just 4 years old. I was fortunate to spend all my childhood years, and part of my teen years, learning from her and growing under her able guardianship.

To begin with, she was the first lady graduate in the state of Mysore, making history. Her life was indeed a shining example, that of a truly emancipated woman, more than a century and a quarter ago when life was much more difficult.

She broke ground for women of the late 19th and early 20th centuries. She challenged the social barriers that prevented women from getting an education.

Here is the story of this iconic personality, a record of her achievements throughout her eventful life.

* * *

As mentioned before, she was born to a Srivaishnava Brahmin couple from a humble background. They worked in the Adiranga temple at Srirangapatna, 18.1 miles from Mysore. Her parents were orthodox and rather conservative. Srirangam went to live with her maternal grandmother Laxmi in Bangalore, under the protection of their maternal uncle, Ramaswamy (Iyengar).

Her grandmother's brother, Ambil Narasimha Iyengar, was extremely compassionate, and generously contributed and supported his sister's entire family, financially and emotionally. He was progressive in his thinking, though he was also from an orthodox Brahmin family. He was a self-made man who valued and respected education.

Initially, he had worked as the young Prince Chamarajendra Wodeyar's, tutor. Later on, he became the Darbar Bakshi, managing the affairs of the entire Mysore Palace. Eventually, he became the adviser to the young King Coronate.

Ambil Narasimha Iyengar observed that young Srirangam was very bright and talented. He initially toyed with the idea of adopting Srirangam to be able to educate her, but respected Srirangam's mother's sentiments. He assured to help her find a suitable groom, and advised Ambuja to move to Mysore

Ambil Narasimha Iyengar arranged a *Vidhyaarambham* (initiation of formal learning) ceremony in Mysore. He coupled the occasion with his *Datthu Sweekara Vidhi* (the adoption ritual). After adopting the 7 or 8-year-old Srirangam, he started tutoring her personally, along with other young girls who came to him to be tutored.

* * *

It is interesting to note that Srirangamma did not stay quiet after her graduation. She emerged as a celebrity in 1903, enjoying the glory of being congratulated by the royal family upon her pioneering graduation. She pursued her post-graduate studies, completing her Honours Degree in English Literature.

By joining the Department of Education workforce on January 16, 1901, she strove relentlessly and toiled hard to better the education standards, especially for girls.

When she realised that parents did not want to send their daughters to schools because there were only male teachers, she started teacher training programmes for young female matriculates, training several female teachers. She also started a small primary school and continued canvassing and enrolling young girls to attend the school regularly.

She went door to door, like a social worker, trying to convince families to send their daughters or teen widows to school, so that they could become literate and educated! She showed great motivation and drive to achieve her goals.

Besides her professional commitments, she did honorary/voluntary work to better the lives of girls by educating them. She took every opportunity she got, and did her best to enhance their socio-economic status.

* * *

It is heartening to see that the educational scenario has changed for the better because of certain specific governmental measures, post India's Independence. Several women and child welfare schemes were introduced to promote the education of women. However, there were many holes in the system which needed immediate and persistent attention, to minimise the dropout rates of girls from schools. On-going interventions helped to reduce the dropout rate significantly, encouraging girls to continue their education and ensure their empowerment.

* * *

An overview of Women's education in India reveals that the goals of education since their inception have changed. A general overview of the status of women's education more than a century after Srirangamma's outstanding and admirable achievements reveals a worrisome picture. Srirangamma too faced challenges as a young student, but she was motivated enough to pursue her education and graduate successfully.

The factors affecting the low literacy rate of girls and young women include social discrimination, gender inequality, domestic responsibilities, and economic exploitation in India (Pallavi Pradeep Purbey, January 3, 2020; A Complete Analysis).

Even after the impressive enrolment following the provision of free and compulsory elementary education, thanks to the Right to Education Act of 2009 introduced by the Government, the following issues contributed to the high drop-out rate among girls:

a.   Poor sanitation facilities, lack of basic sanitation and privacy.
b.   Lack of safe transport to and from school.
c.   Lack of economic opportunity.

Educating women had multiple advantages. If women were educated, it would lead to the country's development. Moreover, educating women would lead to many reforms, and a better understanding of policies launched to address this issue. If women were educated, the nation would have a steady population, and family planning would become a priority, resulting in enhanced awareness. Women would become self-sufficient, and the age at which they got married would probably increase. They would be more independent to take care of their needs and make informed decisions. Women would also be able to handle domestic life, looking after themselves and taking care of the needs of their families.

Women would also better understand their strengths and weaknesses in various aspects of life, and empower themselves to fight for their rights to reduce gender discrepancies, establishing a powerful system in the process. It would also help them voice their opinions.

**Non-profit organisations promoting women's education examined the various causes of poor education for girls in India. Such studies provided insights into the various Government schemes and initiatives launched to address the issue.

The Right to Education Act of 2009 led to an increase in the enrolment of students across the country, along with improved infrastructure and basic civic facilities, thanks to the Sarva Shikshana Abhiyan. However, despite provisions and measures initiated by the Central and state governments to promote education, the dropout rate has been observed to be high (Pallavi Pradeep Purbey, January 3, 2022).

In today's world, there's a keen awareness regarding the need for education. Several initiatives have been implemented around the world to tackle the several problems women face in receiving an education.

After the country won its Independence from British rule, the Government implemented several measures to provide equal opportunities for girls and boys to be educated, and to fight the existing gender discrimination and achieve empowerment. Having equal access to education is crucial to alleviating poverty.

Education also helps strengthen a woman's autonomy, allowing her to marry later, deferring pregnancy and childbirth and improving health. As a consequence, child mortality rates will come down. An educated woman has better opportunities to climb up the corporate ladder. India has done significantly well in providing education to its citizens in the present era.

The Indian Government established many welfare schemes to motivate women to get an education including *Beti Bachao Beti Padao*, Working Women's Hostels, and Support, Training and Employment Programmes (STEP).

The following schemes have had a significant impact on the upliftment of women:

Mahila E-Haat, launched in 2016 by the Ministry of Women's and Children's Development, provides a platform for women entrepreneurs to display and sell their products and services.

Sabla – This scheme was introduced on April 1, 2011, by the former Prime Minister, Rajiv Gandhi, to provide employment for adolescent girls, provide food and nutritional ingredients, facilitate health check-ups, etc.

Swadhar Grah was established in 2002 by the Union Ministry Of Women and Child Development. It provides shelter, food, care, and clothing to unaided women. Women abandoned by their families, and the survivors of any disaster are provided with basic needs.

The One Stop Centre Scheme was introduced in April 2015 by the Ministry of Women and Child Development. It provides counselling services, legal services, police protection, shelter and food to victims of violence.

Nari Shakti Puraskar is an initiative of the Ministry of Women and Child Development to acknowledge and award women for their excellent contribution to society and the empowerment of women.

"The role of women in the new India is continuously expanding," Prime Minister Narendra Modi said on February 1, 2022, as cited in the Times Of India. The Government sought to amend the law to increase the marriageable age of women from 18 to 21 years so that girls could complete their education and build a career. To ensure that marriage at an early age did not hinder the education and career of girls, an effort was being made to raise the marriageable age to 21 years. The Government was committed to a Zero Tolerance Policy with regard to crimes against women, asserting that the participation of women in the growth cycle of New India was essential. The Standing Committee on Education of Women and Children, Youth and Sports (WCYS) was in charge of examining the Bill. The Standing Committee proposed the amendment of the Prohibition Act, 2006.

E-tail giant, Amazon, inked an agreement, Sanjeevini, with the Karnataka State Rural Livelihood Promotion Society [KSRLPS], to promote the market for products of women entrepreneurs and self-help groups. (Cited in the Deccan Herald, Sunday, February 2022).

"This partnership is expected to benefit 30,000 women entrepreneurs, whose products in the categories of groceries, home décor, clothing and others, will be made available to Amazon customers across India. The agreement was inked in the presence of the Chief Minister and senior Amazon representatives. Amazon will not only launch the Sanjeevini Programme, but will also extend the benefits to the Saheli Programme, to train and empower thousands of women entrepreneurs to go on-line and access a wider market for their products. The state envisages increased visibility for the woman entrepreneur's products."

There are various organisations promoting women's education in India. These entities fight against gender inequalities while emphasising the importance of women's education in India.

Some of the non-profit entities that promote girls' education are:

Educate Girls Bond which creates new opportunities for the education of girls and promotes gender equality.

Grassroots is an entity that promotes leadership among women and girls in the community, by employing mindfulness tactics to reach social resolutions.

Pratham is designed to improve the education of girls in Mumbai.

Campaign For Female Education (CAMFE) is an international non-profit organisation helping marginalised girls succeed through education.

Girls Who Code (GWC) is an international non-profit organisation that aims to support and increase the number of women in computer science.

* * *

The following anecdote dates back to the latter part of the 20th century, around 1996-97.

Refreshingly enough, there are instances of private individuals who have taken initiatives in the direction of educating, protecting, nurturing and empowering girls. One such example is a highly professional couple who had the courage and compassion to raise and nurture young girl babies, and educate them too!

Disha, a girls' home, was set up by a private couple, Dr. Rama Deshpande and Dr. Ramakrishna Nayak. It was started under the auspices of the Gundbala Welfare Trust in 1997 when Dr. Deshpande worked as a Secretary to the Education Welfare Public Trust. When the couple was in the process of adopting their second child, they became aware of three to four abandoned baby girls. The babies became the wards of the Secretary of the Trust, by the order of the court.

The Nayaks began to care for and nurture the babies in their home in Ankola. Dr. Rama gave up her job to take personal care of the babies in Disha. The fourth orphaned girl was also given shelter and education. She eventually reunited with her maternal grandmother.

The Nayaks loved and cared for the babies, and provided early stimulation and nutrition throughout their growing years, besides instilling moral values in them, and giving them a good education. The three girls grew up with the Nayak's two children, a biological son and an adopted daughter. They all enjoyed an enriched childhood. The three girls grew into poised women, educated, employed, married and well-settled.

I want the world to know how unassuming individuals and families voluntarily strive in their own capacities, to devote their lives towards educating, emancipating and empowering girls. They deserve to enjoy a deep sense of satisfaction.

* * *

The online portal, Women's Web, carried a story in April, 2018, about five amazing women in the education sector who reached out to students.

We have come a long way from women being deprived of education to having some revolutionary women in the educational arena in India. Our country boasts several people who have selflessly done whatever they could for the betterment of society. Illiteracy among women is still a serious problem, not only in India but also worldwide. Some women have taken on the responsibility of changing this scenario.

What makes them extraordinary is the compassion that they exhibit towards other humans. They work relentlessly to help others, rather than live their own lives. Here, I'm tempted to include my grandmother Srirangamma among those ladies who have worked selflessly, doing everything in their capacity to propagate the education of girls.

A) At age 81, Vimala Kaul, who had been a teacher all her life, worked in Guldastha, her own school established for underprivileged children. Post-retirement, she chose to teach children from the slums.

B) Roshni Mukherjee established Exam Fear Education, quitting a well-paying IT company. She was always a good student and had a passion for teaching. She decided to run a virtual school on the internet, reaching thousands of students who were keen to learn worldwide. She realised that the internet had the power to reach every nook and corner of the world. Her teaching methods are simple. She explains the concepts of Physics, Chemistry, Maths and Biology using examples from daily life. She uses pictures and animation to simplify concepts.

C) Geeta Dharmarajan is also a teacher, an author of children's books, an editor, a social worker, and a Padmashree Awardee! She established Katha 28 years ago, and today, Katha runs schools for underprivileged children in 252 slums. She began publishing Tamasha, a children's magazine, with colourful illustrations and stories on health, the environment and empowering women. She helps women by training them in vocations such as cooking, baking and embroidery, to enable them to earn a supplementary monthly income of Rs 1000, so that they can send their children to the Katha school. Currently, Katha's students are pursuing professions like Medicine, Engineering and Teaching!

D) Vasudha Prakash was pursuing her Doctorate studies in the USA, focusing on special schooling in India. She became aware of the dearth of schools for children with special needs in India. She founded Excel, a learning centre which teaches medicine, vocational and educational skills to persons with special needs. She started the school with 11 students, and currently has 3500 students across the nation!

Vasudha insists that Government schools must employ inclusive education. Along with her staff, she trains schools to implement inclusive education. She sensitises students to be aware and tolerant of special children. She also teaches special children, social skills.

E) Muktha Doghli had lost her sight due to Meningitis as a child. She pursued a Diploma in teacher training for the blind and earned a B.A. Degree with First Class. She aspired to do something for the blind, especially for blind women. She started a non-profit school for the blind and visually impaired in 1995 in Gujarat. So far, 400 students have graduated from the institute, equipped with various skills including coding in different languages, and teaching Braille. Some have even become Electrical Engineers, Beauticians, and Chefs.

Mukthaben trains students to be fearless and self-confident. She facilitated the marriages of couples with visual deficiencies. She and her husband decided not to have biological children, but they adopted blind girls and gave them a better life.

The online portal Women's Web has listed a few noteworthy women in the educational field who have founded schools to make children literate so that they can get employed, and earn a living for themselves and their families.

These revolutionary women in the educational field have silently changed the educational platform for marginalised children. Don't you think that the world needs to know about the work of these inconspicuous heroes?

Initially, the Government of India focussed on educating girls. It implemented several measures to safeguard education as a fundamental right and aimed to protect these rights. It ensured that all girls got a minimum standard of education. In recent years, the goal has changed from women's development to women-led development.

This anecdote illustrates how the importance of women's education and empowerment has been globally recognised as crucial, and several programmes have been launched towards this end. Carla Koppel of the

United States Agency for International Development (USAID) even called Education a Silver Bullet for empowerment and progress.

Education has the following impact on society:

1. Increased literacy: By offering all children education, the literacy rate of the country is increased, hiking up development, especially in the struggling regions of the world.

2. Human Trafficking: Women are most vulnerable to trafficking when they are undereducated and poor, according to the United Nation's Inter-Agency Project on Human Trafficking. Through providing opportunities and fundamental skills, this social evil can be crippled.

3. Political Representation: Across the globe, women are under-represented as voters, and are restricted from political involvement. The United Nations Programmes on leadership and participation supports that civic education and training will ease this gap.

4. Thriving babies: According to United Nations Girls Education Initiatives, children of educated mothers are twice as likely to survive past the age of 5 years. Foreign aid for schoolhouses, and curriculum development could greatly benefit the East African Country of Burundai, where numerous babies die every year.

5. Later Marriage: As suggested by the United Nations Population Fund, in underprivileged countries, one in every three girls is married before the age of 18 years. In regions where girls receive seven or more years of education, marriage is delayed by four years.

6. Smaller Families: Increased participation in school, reduces fertility rate over time. Mature women, who have completed their secondary education or higher, have an average of three children. Women with no education have an average of seven children.

7. Income Potential: Education also empowers the woman's wallet by boosting economic potential. According to the United Nations Economic and Scientific Organisation (UNESCO), a single year of primary education has seen an increase in a girl's wages later in life by 20%.

8. Thriving Gross Domestic Product (GDP): GDP scores when girls and boys are offered educational opportunities. When 10 % more women attend school, the GDP increases by 3%, on average.

9. Poverty Reduction: When women are provided equal rights and equal access to education, they participate in business and economic activity. Increased earning power allows them to combat current and future poverty through feeding, clothing and providing for the entire family.

"The sustainability and progress of all regions depend on the success of women across the globe. The future must not belong to those who bully women. It must be shaped by those who go to school, and those who stand for a world where our daughters can live their dreams, just like our sons," President Obama said while addressing the UN General Assembly in 2012.

Do you understand the important and powerful role Education plays in the development of a country?

Education is the most powerful weapon which you can use to change the world – Nelson Mandela.

* * *

It is indeed interesting to recognise that the goals of education have changed in the years after the inception of the initial governmental policy. The Karnataka Policy of Empowerment 2018 emphasised the equality of women which included several basic rights of women. It included women's right to live with dignity, the right to a sense of self-worth, the right to determine choice, the right to opportunities and resources, and the right to control their own lives! It also included the ability to influence the direction of social and economic order.

As per the State Policy Of Empowerment, increased awareness has inspired women to leave their homes and care for their own emotional, spiritual, religious and economic needs. Women have now become a tool for change in India.

Despite the increased freedom they enjoy, women still experience constraints because of patriarchal prejudices that tend to linger in society. Though the status of women is perceived to be high, the overall picture is questionable in reality.

The education of women should mean the narrowing down of social disparities and gender inequalities. Social reformers and researchers state that despite drastic changes brought about in society, women continue to struggle against the deep-rooted patriarchal mentality. Dr. Maniwal Sujatha, Assistant Professor of Sociology, Department of Sociology, Meerut, has studied" the changing status of women, in modern India." She states, "Equal footing with men is still an illusion for females because male domination still prevails."[p283,289-290](Praveen Kumar Kulkarni, History of Women's Education in India – Article Library).

World-renowned Anthropologist, Dr. M.N. Srinivas (Srirangamma's nephew), in his studies, *Changing Status of Indian Women*, describes the position of modern women. He states, "The obviously changing position of modern women participating in politics and social reforms has impacted the role of women, although to a limited extent, thus benefitting only a few women." (August 1977, Published by Royal Anthropological New Series, Vol 12 – p 221-228, Institute Of Great Britain, Ireland).

Thus, despite ample measures and initiatives taken by the Government to promote education and uplift women, their social status has not improved much as a result of lingering gender biases and male domination!

* * *

Smt. Srirangamma was a poised, independent and modern lady way ahead of her time. She challenged traditional restrictions, empowering and emancipating herself, and inspiring other women to do the same. She was confident and adventurous enough to take initiatives to better her own life, to be resourceful, to take risks, to learn new tasks, and to steer her own life till she was in her eighties. She was self-aware and planned her life with discretion. She helped to better the lives of women who needed support. She also mobilised change for the better.

She was popular among women, many of whom approached her to seek her advice. She was easily accessible and was referred to as *Akkayya* (revered big sister/didi).

She dedicated her life to creating subtle changes for the better in society. She trained many women to be teachers. She also provided vocational training where women could work as nurses or midwives. In this way, she empowered young widows to leave the confines of their dark attics and basements and lead emancipated lives.

Srirangamma seems to have followed the footsteps of her father, Sri Ambil Narasimha Iyengar, and his friend Sri M. Venkatakrishnaiah, who were her early role models. She was fondly called 'teacher' by many women who came to her to learn.

I heard many personal stories from individuals who placed their hands on my head in 1981, showering me with blessings, when I had just started Kreedangana, my preschool. They elaborated on how their 'Madam' had lit the lamp of their life by educating them, thereby making their lives meaningful.

Srirangamma derived her own value system, stood up for her convictions and principles, and set an example for the younger members of her family who imbibed these values. She felt proud when she recognised the strength of character in the younger members of her family.

She also felt sad and disappointed when they failed to imbibe the values she considered important. When they failed to empower themselves, became subservient, and were tolerant of discrimination, deprivation, obsessive patriarchal dominance and abuse, despite their self-awareness and education, she became despondent.

She was fully aware that every individual had to strive hard, earn and give themselves certain gifts, know their self-worth and command respect for themselves. However sincere and fervent her intentions were, she couldn't spoon-feed or inject these precious commodities to other women. Mere literacy and a university degree alone didn't guarantee all these fringe benefits. Srirangamma, however, strove relentlessly to steer social change at every opportunity she got to promote a more just social and economic order.

Srirangamma celebrated her 83rd birthday on August 11, 1958. Subsequently, she suffered from age-related health issues. In 1958, she travelled to attend the A I W Conference but was not able to participate much in the fieldwork. She passed away on February 13, 1959, after a brief heart ailment. She has left behind a rich legacy such that she will live in our hearts forever.

A retrospective overview of Smt. Srirangamma's entire life, in light of the principles of gender equality and empowerment, as laid down by the state policy, allows us to fully appreciate how empowered and emancipated she evolved to be over a century ago!

Srirangamma was strong and stable under changing circumstances, in the face of challenges galore, including intense grief, emotional vulnerability, shocks and surprises. As a young lady, she remained poised under various trying situations and maintained her individuality, dignity, composure, and indomitable spirit. She maintained her composure and strength of character, even as she aged gracefully.

She was consistently confident and adventurous enough to take the initiative to better her life and to be resourceful.

Changing Goals of Women's Education in India

Education is obviously the stepping stone to women's empowerment.

"…and the evidence shows that when the communities give their daughters the same opportunities as their sons, they are more powerful, they are more prosperous, they develop faster, and they are more likely to succeed," Barak Obama said.

Women's education is very relevant to a country's progress and development. It is interesting to note that the goals of women's education at its inception in the 1880s in Mysore, were only limited to preparing girls for marriage and orienting them to adapt better to married life, as decided by the elite male members of our orthodox society! So, when Maharani's Girls School was first established in Mysore, the curriculum introduced suited the initial goal of education. As the school progressed, changes were incorporated to continue educating girls for life.

Women's education got a fillip after Independence in 1947, when the Government introduced various measures to ensure education to all women, with its own goals and expectations. Well-known social reformers also played a major role in promoting gender equality and girls' education, including Madhav Govind Ranade, Rajaram Mohan Roy, and Ishwar Chandra Vidhya Sagar. They deserve our appreciation for their contributions towards girls' education.

Dr. Ambedkar also focussed on women's education and empowerment. "I measure the progress of any country by the degree of progress women have achieved." "The state shall not deny to any person, equality before the law or the equal protection of the laws, within the territory of India." (The Hindu Code Bill – Dr. Ambedkar).

Women's empowerment is the progression of accepting and including women in the decision-making process. It also means providing them with equal opportunities for growth and development in society and disapproving of gender biases.

As regards the welfare of women and children, Article 15(3) states that "Nothing in the Article, shall prevent the state from making any state provision for women and children."

Women and children are recognised not only as a vital part of society but also as the most valuable sections of India. The Article provides a list of empowerment schemes in India as listed under the Ministry of Women and Children's Development.

Here is a list of the major women's empowerment schemes in India:

According to recent news, Minister of Women And Child Welfare, Smriti Irani, speaking at the 25th Anniversary of the 4th Women's Conference at the United Nations said that India recognised the centrality of gender equality and women's empowerment in all aspects of development.

She highlighted that more than 200 million women have been brought under the formal banking system through the Government's Financial Inclusive Initiative. The innovative use of digital technologies has provided equal opportunities for women to access insurance, loans and social assistance.

Microsoft recently announced that it has collaborated with National Skill Development (NSDC) to impart digital skills to more than 1 lakh underprivileged, and underserved women in India. This initiative is an extension of the Microsoft Partnership with NSDC, to provide digital skills to 1 lakh youth in the country. The programme will create a series of live training sessions and digital skilling drives to provide opportunities to young girls and women, particularly first-time job seekers, and those whose jobs may have been impacted by COVID-19, to get them ready for employment.

In recent times, women's empowerment in India is increasingly receiving more attention. One NGO is working to help disadvantaged Indian women achieve financial independence through an all-women's cab company. The Azad Foundation's Women on Wheels programme empowers impoverished women in India, by providing them with a stable source of income and a safe environment, where they can travel without the fear of being harassed.

Education plays a crucial role in building self-confidence in a woman. It also boosts her status, in society. It enables her to build confidence to make informed decisions. Up-skilling and micro-financing can provide women with financial stability where they are not dependent on others. Educating women actually means ensuring that the entire family is educated.

The Constitution of India has certain provisions that focus on women's empowerment, and aim to prevent discrimination against women.

Article 14 talks about the equality of women before the law.

Article 15 enables the state to make special provisions for women. As the progress of humanity is incomplete without women, successive Governments have launched several schemes for the empowerment of women in a rather male-dominated society.

Beti Bachao, Beti Padao was launched to create awareness among people to educate every girl child in the country. The Government has successfully promoted this scheme by forming the District Task Force and Block Task Force. This scheme was formed in 2015 in Panipat, Haryana, and the child sex ratio has increased since its inception. There was massive publicity for this programme.

Both earning a living and education are important factors for the empowerment of women. An unskilled labourer is not empowered even though she is employed. Despite education, a woman cannot be empowered if she is unemployed and not earning. So, financial independence is crucial for empowerment. Women who are educated and employed are in a much better position in our society when compared to uneducated women.

Working Women's Hostel was launched to ensure special and convenient accommodation for working women. Any woman can benefit from this scheme regardless of caste, religion or marital status. Those earning a total gross income of less than Rs 50,000 a month are eligible for such accommodation in a metropolitan city. Those with a total gross income of less than Rs 35000 a month in small cities can avail of this scheme.

The Convention on the Elimination of all Forms of Discrimination Against Women (CEDAW) is an international legal instrument that requires countries to eliminate discrimination against women and girls in all areas and promotes equal rights for women and girls. CEDAW is often described as the international bill of rights for women and is one of the key international agreements that guides the work of UN Women in achieving gender equality and empowering all women and girls. (Source: unwomen. org). India has reconfirmed and agreed to CEDAW for the upliftment of women.

Of late, the focus of the Government of India has shifted from women's development to women-led development. To achieve this goal, the Government is trying to maximise every woman's access to education, skill training and institutional credit. P.M. Narendra Modi, while charting the New India growth story, has emphasised that India is transitioning its focus from women's development to women-led development.

With this special perspective, women are considered as able architects of India's progress and development. They are no longer looked upon as passive recipients of the fruits of the country's development. Here, the true potential of women is acknowledged, and hence, they are empowered to justify their role. With this view, the focus has been on enhancing facilities to ensure their nutrition, health and empowerment needs.

In 2017, the Government launched the *Pradhan Manthri Mathru Vandhana Yojana* towards meeting women's needs.

Under the Swatch Bharath mission, more toilets were built in collaboration with UNICEF, to ensure safety, convenience and self-respect for women in rural India in 2020.

Jan Dhan Yojana plays a major role in making formal banking and financial services accessible to women.

Kushal Vikas Yojana is a Government of India initiative which promotes self-employment through training for women.

Micro Units Development and Refinance Agency (MUDRA Yojana) is one such scheme launched on April 8, 2015, in which grants of loans up to Rs 10 lakhs are made available to women entrepreneurs, free of collateral.

In the past, several women had to inevitably give up their jobs after childbirth, resulting in their unemployment. Of late, the government has passed the Maternity Benefit (Amendment) Act 2017, increasing the period of maternity leave from 12 weeks to 26 weeks. This is also part of the P.M. Pradhan Manthri Mathru Vandhana Yojana.

Occupational Safety, Health and Working Condition Code, 2020, envisages the employment of women. It works on exempting women from night duty and ensuring gender equality in a big way.

Prime Minister Narendra Modi has also expressed the importance of women's empowerment in the 82nd edition of *Mann Ki Baat*, (his broadcasted speech on AIR, on the fourth Sunday of every month). He has acknowledged and commended the increase in the fleet of women police personnel in the country when compared to the figures in 1914.

Considering these measures, has Prime Minister Modi's vision proved to be revolutionary? Has it also helped to make women a leading force?

* * *

Please find below a host of influential ladies in the field of education.

Since women are considered the building blocks of the nation, empowering women is similar to empowering the nation. Indian women have made us proud in every aspect. We have a host of women who have excelled in almost every field of expertise.

a. Avani Chaturvedi is the first Indian woman fighter pilot to fly a MiG-21.

b. Manika Batra is the top-ranked woman table tennis player in India.

c. Gita Gopinath is the first Indian appointed as Chief Economist at the International Monitory Fund (IMF)

d. Hema Das is the first Indian woman athlete who won the Gold Medal at the International Association of Athletics Federations (IAAF) Under 20 Championship.

e. Mangte Chungneijang Mary Kom is the only woman to have won the World Amateur Boxing Championship.

f. Padmasree Warrior, the former Cisco CTO, made it to America's top woman in tech according to Forbes magazine.

g. Seema Rao is India's first woman commando trainer, who is also known as India's Wonder Woman.

h. Komal Mangtani is the world's first and most influential woman software engineer who heads the Business Intelligence Team at Uber.

i. Bachendri Pal was rewarded a Gold Medal by the Indian Mountaineering Foundation, for Excellence in Mountaineering. She received the Padma Shri, the 4th highest civilian award in 1984. She also received the Padma Bhushan, the third-highest civilian award of the Republic Of India.

j. D. Roopa, is currently the Inspector General of Police. This Bengaluru tough cop released a music video to inspire women on International Women's Day, 2018.

k. Kala Ramachandran is the first Woman Commissioner of Police in Gurugram, as on February 15, 2022.

There are a host of other women who have empowered themselves, making a difference in the lives of others. These individuals make the nation proud. If women are strong and capable of withstanding any storm, they will rule the world. We need to treat such women with utmost dignity, in all spheres of life, to build a most influential and powerful country. The new strategies and initiatives like socio-cultural practices promote women's education by introducing social empowerment tools with access to education, healthcare, and equal opportunities. (Pallavi Pradeep Purbey, January 3, 2022, Women's Education In India – A Complete Analysis.)

It is a matter of great pride for India when it comes to the women behind the launch of the Chandrayan 3. This mission, launched by the Indian Space Research Organisation (ISRO), boasts the participation of several women scientists in high positions including project managers and directors at various centres. Ritu Karidhal, an aerospace engineer at ISRO and India's Rocket Woman, is a shining example of the power of dreams and determination. Other renowned women who made substantial contributions to the Chandrayan 3 Mission include Anuradha T.K., M. Valamathi, Mangala Mani, Mamtha Datta, Nandini Harinath, Meenakshi Sampoorneshwari, Keerti Aujdar, and Tessy Thomas.

Altogether, 75 engineers of India were recognised, appreciated and honoured by the Indian National Academy of Engineering. Dr. Dheepa Srinivasan is recognised as the pioneer in additives manufacturing and for enabling indigenous development. She received the Women Engineers 2020 Award. She is passionate about indigenous technology development and bringing more women into STEM.

She is the chief engineer at Pratt and Whitney R.D. Centre at the IISc campus. She has over 35 patents in her name and has developed more than 50 technologies and process applications that are being used to run several gas and steam turbines. The scientists and engineers will be honoured in a ceremony that will be held in December 2023.

Dr. Shantala Hari Dass completed her Ph.D from NTU, Singapore, in neuroscience.

She pursued a post-doctorate degree at McGill, Canada. Her research stints across continents have produced almost 20 publications. Until recently, she worked as the Executive Director of IndiaBioscience, Bangalore. Currently, she is Communicative Manager at Canada's National Platform for Genome Sequencing and Analysis. She works with sick kids at a renowned hospital employing 2000 genomic researchers across Canada. She enables these complex research findings to reach non-experts and stakeholders across communities, including the government.

"It's impossible to think about the welfare of the world unless the condition of women is improved," said Swami Vivekananda. (Status of Women During British Rule).

The above-mentioned individuals have contributed to the wellbeing of the nation. By mere virtue of their strength, they are capable of withstanding any storm, and they have everything it takes to rule the world. They need and deserve to be treated with utmost dignity in all spheres of life, to build a most influential and powerful country.

Birds of the Same Feather Flock Together

This anecdote dates back to the late 1800s. The Women's Education Movement was initiated by different people in different parts of India, including Maharashtra, Karnataka, Bengal, Mysore, Kerala and Tamil Nadu. It is interesting to observe that the champions of education, by coincidence, found people with similar goals, or similar calibre of commitment, to pursue their objectives. They worked together, facing similar challenges. They all seemed to have enjoyed the comradeship!

Mahatma Jyotirao Phule had a vision to educate girls. He happened to recognise a relationship of comradeship with his wife, Savitribai, and he educated her, enlisting her as part of his team to educate girls.

This Mother of women's education teamed up with Fatima Sheikh and her brother Usman Sheikh, and they started the very first girls' school ever in the latter's residence, called The Indigenous Library in 1848! Fatima also offered refuge to Jyotirao when he was forced to leave his home in Pune, for challenging the norms and educating Dalit girls. Fatima Sheikh challenged both the upper caste Hindu men and orthodox Muslims as well. (History of the Education of Girls in India, Your Article Library... January 3, 2021).

Anandi Gopal Joshi was herself a pioneer who graduated when no women ever went to school or was educated. She asserted her right to admission, based on eligibility and set a precedence for the admission of girls to school, to be educated henceforth. Anandi was a contemporary of Kadambini Ganguly, and Chandramukhi Basu, both of whom graduated as medical doctors in Calcutta.

Anandi was married when she was 9 years old to Gopal Joshi, 20 years older than her. At age 14, she gave birth to a baby boy who died early due to lack of medical care. This infanticide and her own experience of lack of adequate medical care in India inspired her to pursue a medical degree. She applied to the Women's Medical College Of Pennsylvania, USA. She was a pioneer who graduated in 1886. Her thesis utilised references from both American and Ayurvedic texts.

She received congratulatory messages from Queen Victoria upon her graduation. She became the first Indian lady doctor and returned to India, and received a grand welcome. The princely state of Kolhapur appointed her as the physician in charge of the female ward of the local Albert Edward Hospital. Ironically, Anandibai died of tuberculosis in 1887 at the young age of 22 years. Despite having been able to practice medicine for only a couple of months, she rose to fame for her sheer resolve, grit and hard work to become a pioneer, and to study Western medicine. She instantly became a source of inspiration to all others who came after her. (Here is How Anandibai Joshi Became India's First Female Doctor – Tashafi Nazir, February 26, 2022).

Ramabai was born into a Maratha speaking Chithpavan Brahmin family. Calcutta University conferred upon her the titles Pandita and Sarasvati, in recognition of her vast knowledge of various Sanskrit works and scripts. She was a social reformer, besides being a knowledgeable educator. She moved to Pune in 1882 and founded an organisation to promote women's education. She also founded the Arya Mahila Samaj, the purpose of which was the education of women and the prevention of child marriage. Ramabai travelled to Britain in 1883 to pursue a medical degree. Due to her progressive deafness, she was rejected in 1886.

She travelled to the United States at the invitation of the Dean of Women's Medical College of Pennsylvania, to attend the graduation of her cousin, the pioneering medical doctor, Anandi Gopal Joshi. In 1887, Ramabai published her first English book, *The High-Caste Hindu Women*, a merciless indictment of India's treatment of Hindu women. Upon her return to India, she opened an institute for the education of young widows in Bombay. *Mukti* (salvation), the famous orphanage was started in 1898. She wrote the forward to the book, *More About Anandibai Joshi*, on the title page of her own book and signed it in 1886. The title page to this rare signed copy reads, "The High-Caste Hindu Women and Society," by Pandita Ramabai Sarasvati, with an introduction by Rachel L Bodley, AMMD, Dean of Women's Medical College of Pennsylvania, Ten Thousand, Philadelphia, 1888.

Chandramukhi Basu and Kadambini Ganguli were the first women medical students of Bethune College in Calcutta. Kadambini Ganguli was an accomplished professional in the 19th century in British India. A pioneer in many spheres, Kadambini Ganguli was the first woman to practice Western medicine and to attend medical college in India. Chandramukhi Basu was another pioneer who graduated in British India in 1882, along with the former, from the University of Calcutta.

We have seen how Ambil Narasimha Iyengar and Sri Venkatakrishnaiah strove to be pioneers and initiated a school exclusively for girls in Mysore around the 1880s. Obviously, the two gentlemen seemed to have enjoyed a comradeship in pursuing their mission.

Smt. Srirangamma was a pioneer who took the initiative to educate herself despite the numerous challenges she faced and succeeded in graduating from Maharani's High School, Mysore. She pursued her undergraduate studies at Central College, Bangalore, and graduated in 1903. She pursued her postgraduate degree and got her Honours in English Literature, despite the numerous challenges. Her paternal aunt, K.D. Rukmaniamma, completed her graduation in Mysore after Maharani High School was upgraded to a second grade college. Ms Subbamma followed suit and completed her Panditha exam. Madras Presidency announced the graduation of the three pioneering ladies in 1906.

It is obvious that most of the pioneering individuals gravitated towards others with similar goals. Together they invested their energies in their joint ventures.

(1) కీర్తిశేషురాలయిన సుబ్బమ్మగారు బి. ఏ.

(2) శ్రీమతి శ్రీరంగమ్మగారు బి. ఏ.

(3) శ్రీమతి యక్ష్మణమ్మగారు బి. ఏ.

Amba, My Dear Grandmother, Or Was She My Godmother?

Amba was my cuddly grandmother, Srirangamma, on whose lap I grew up and blossomed as a child. I often wondered if she was real, if she was my Fairy Godmother, just like Cinderella's Fairy Godmother.

Why I chose to call her Amba, I am not aware of. I do remember that Hindu goddesses are also addressed as Amba. I do not remember any adult at home who could have prompted or suggested that I call her Amba.

For me, Amba was there by my side every single moment, to quell my fears, wipe my tears, hold my hand, and reassure me. Her warm arms around me made me feel not only safe but also special, as if I was her princess!

Once, I went screaming to her, afraid of a spider that was crawling near me! She held me and pacified me, explaining that spiders were friendly creatures. I am not sure if she had succeeded in convincing me about the spider's friendly intentions. I brought my book of nursery rhymes, showed her a picture and recited a familiar rhyme:

"Little Miss Muffet, sat on a tuffet, eating her curds and whey.

There came a spider, sat down beside her, and frightened Miss Muffet away!"

Amba was quick-witted. She quickly brought out a puppet of an old lady and said, "Out came grandma and shoo shooed the spider away." Amba sure knew how to reassure a scared young child.

I was 4 years old around this time and about as tall as her thighs. Amba often watched me from close quarters with great care, and showed gentle appreciation in her beautiful smile. I loved her silky silver hair that shone in the daylight! She never spared an opportunity to tell me that soon I would achieve great things. She often appreciated how softly I spoke to everyone at home. She often encouraged me to speak fluently without any hesitation.

She introduced me to the science of plants and taught me how to identify herbs and weeds by the shapes and patterns of the leaves. When I was barely 6 or 7 years old, I could name many flowers, and recognise herbs and shrubs by their names. I could recognise and name all the fruit trees, and a couple of flowering trees in her vast garden, based on their leaves and bark.

Amba told me that the hibiscus was the perfect flower. She showed me the distinct parts of the flower. I learned the right way to cut roses early in life. She took me along to Lalbagh, where she attended a workshop on grafting rose buds, and air layering native hibiscus plants. I was very proud when I planted a French Pink Rose, *La France*, and it bloomed!

Amba gradually established a routine for me, quite early in life. Every morning, she would wake me up early and would teach me to sing and play the Veena (a string instrument), on the same Veena she had used as a child. After letting me take a nap on her warm lap, she would wake me up again. She would get me to brush my teeth and freshen up for an English language lesson.

She would teach me to write sentences. On some days it would be purely grammar lessons. Gradually, she introduced me to the dictionary and helped me find the meaning of new words. Later on, we would have discussions during which she would encourage me to use the new words I had learned. She often complimented me on my impressive vocabulary. I noted down all the new words I had learned in a diary.

After school, I would sit on the sturdy handles of her recliner chair, and request her to tell me her story, or talk about Ambil *Thatha's* challenges.

She would tell me detailed accounts of her experiences over and over again.

* * *

Here is an anecdote Amba shared with me about her early childhood in Srirangapatnam, when I was around 6 or 7 years old. We had travelled by train to Srirangapatnam and had just disembarked. Amba talked to a Tonga driver and hired him to take us to the Adi Ranga Temple where her parents had worked when she was a child. We enjoyed the temple visit. My mother explained to me that the temple walls had murals of Lord Krishna's childhood experiences.

We had lunch at the temple and went to the River Kaveri. *Amma* let my niece, Geeta, and me splash about in the waters, under her supervision. We had a lot of fun. Amba wrote our names in the wet sand with her forefinger and showed us how she had learned her first lessons on the wet river sand. Geeta and I built sand castles and a fort with river pebbles.

She took me in the tonga (horse-drawn cart) to the street where her parents had lived in a row of homes amidst the community of orthodox Brahmins who were mostly temple staff. These houses had huge pillars in front and beautiful carved wooden doors, like the ones at the temple! There was a bronze bell hung to the right side of the entrance. I wanted to ring the bell and made a request. I was lifted so that I could ring the bell. Some very nice people opened the door and ushered us in with a lot of respect. They offered us buttermilk and fruits. It was such a memorable visit, a crucial part of my childhood.

* * *

As I grew taller and older, Amba spared no chance to teach me. She often told me that in writing, there were several opportunities to talk about any topic. "The sky is the limit," she would say, to remind me of the unending possibilities. She often encouraged me to write by suggesting various topics and writing soon became a hobby for me. She would hold my hands and gently talk to me as she explained things. She taught me spoken English, English grammar, Arithmetic, and Science.

She taught me how to clean the front porch every morning, and decorate it with a small Rangoli. I was entrusted with the responsibility of creating this welcome symbol every morning. She usually explained the cultural significance of the rituals we followed, instead of forcing us to follow traditions blindly. The Rangoli is a welcome symbol for visitors.

Amba introduced me to the art of sewing and taught me the rudiments of basic embroidery when I was just a child. She first discussed the safety rules and taught me how to take care of the accessories. She explained the importance of knotting the rear end of the thread, and how not to misplace or lose the needle.

Amba bought fabric, coloured threads, and sewing kits and undertook small sewing projects. She took me to the store to identify various accessories like beads, laces, bells, and mirror pieces and encouraged me to make creative gifts for my cousins and friends. She was proud to share my creative projects with her friends and family.

Like an excellent teacher, she began teaching me life skills, including how to manage money, when I was barely 10 years old. She started by giving me pocket money of Rs 5 each month. She encouraged me to spend and manage my money, keep accounts and save whatever I could.

Every Wednesday we would visit the post office to buy stamps to mail a letter to my brother who was working in Lebanon. She introduced me to the art of letter writing and encouraged me to write a letter every week to my brother, telling him all about school, and other activities.

At the end of each school year, she would take Geeta and me to a famous stationery store. There, we could choose any art accessories that we wanted as a reward for being promoted to a higher class. This was an opportunity to use my savings on a special purchase. Sometimes, I would buy something special for Geeta and she would in turn gift me something.

She taught me some simple crafts using natural objects, such as making *thoranas* (decorative garlands) by weaving mango and neem leaves on twine. The garlands would be used to decorate the entrance on special days and festivals. I was very proud to have made my own leaf plate and bowl using jackfruit tree leaves, stitching them together with thin split sticks! I was also taught to make garlands using varieties of jasmine blossoms and scented herbs.

Ever since I was about 10 or 11 years old, Geeta and I were encouraged to have our own small kitchen garden beds to sow vegetables and grow beans, carrots, small tomatoes, ginger and turmeric roots. We had child-friendly shovels, rakes, watering cans and tiny buckets to water mint, basil and other medicinal herbs.

Geeta and I had the privilege of learning how to use sandpaper on small furniture like racks, bookends, and key-stands at an early age. We learned to follow the safety rules, wash our hands, clean the accessories after use, and safeguard them. The following summer, we learned how to varnish furniture.

I escorted Amba to Bombay and Poona annually, when she had to attend the All India Women's Conference. I would hold her hand and travel with her by Western Railways. She made train travel exciting and interesting, teaching me how to read signs and familiarising me with the names of each station en route. I also observed the different accents of vendors and porters in different stations. I became aware of the voice modulation of the vendors who routinely sold coffee, tea, biscuits and other snacks. I learned to read railway travel books to keep track of the names of stations. Eventually, I learned to read railway route maps as well. Soon, I learned to be responsible and keep track of our luggage, especially when we had to change trains at the Guntakal Junction.

My Experiences of Starting and Running a Preschool – Kreedangan/Kreeda Ranga

This section is all about a preschool that I was fortunate to start in 1981 on my grandmother Srirangamma's property. I grew up with my grandmother, watching her work and listening to stories about her achievements. This inspired me to accomplish something special in life.

Amidst the challenges of my times, I successfully pursued my Master's Degree in Early Childhood Development, and Early Childhood Education from M.S. University, Baroda, Gujarat.

Having worked in a reputed school in Bangalore as a founder teacher, I was involved in spade work, overall planning, developing the curriculum and hands-on activities to stimulate primary school children. I had always dreamed of starting a school as a child and I was fortunate to have this dream come true. I kept gathering a wide range of skill sets and experiences, till personal circumstances and family commitments were conducive to venture into a creative workspace.

I started Kreedangan in October 1981 under a tree, in the style of Rabindranath Tagore's Santiniketan, with just nine children. Although I had a venue, I had no money and nobody to help. But my heart was full of lofty ideas. I invited a childhood friend, Vijaya, to be by my side in this adventure. All that I could offer her was to take care of her transport expenses and provide free childcare for her toddler.

Kreedangan started out as an inclusive preschool, with the very first toddler enrolled being visually impaired! Later, a pre-schooler with cerebral palsy was also admitted. I was able to handle these youngsters with special needs only because of my background, having trained and worked in an Infant Stimulation Programme of the Easter Seals Society, in Maui, Hawaii, USA, in 1973.

I had the golden opportunity in Maui to work with a rich team of experts in the federally funded programme which took a multi-disciplinary approach to development. The team consisted of paediatricians, neurologists, nurses, speech specialists, physiotherapists, preschool staff, and social workers in a mobile preschool set up for toddlers with delayed milestones.

I was extremely blessed to have the invaluable moral support of my sister's family, of Geeta, of my adopted parents, the Sharmas, and my aunt Smt. G.S. Lalitha. Aunty Lalitha and Anita Sharma were trained to head my preschool and manage and develop it whenever I travelled abroad.

My brother Narendra and his family generously permitted me to use the premises free of rent for the first six years. Later, they accepted only a token rent. I trained all my teaching staff and helpers to be sensitive to the needs of these special children and to be generously patient.

Eventually, Kreedangan Pre-school was revamped, and renamed as Kreedaranga (A Stage for Play), and was dedicated to Srirangamma. I was certainly blessed to enjoy the creative and challenging experience of establishing and running the preschool for 35 years!

Kreedaranga also had an inclusive preschool feature where a few children with delayed milestones due to autism, Down's syndrome, seizures, developmental delays, speech delays, and severe attention deficit disorder attended school along with normal pre-schoolers. All the children were exposed to maximum opportunities for muscular coordination, overall stimulation, and attention retention activities using music, movement, and multi-sensory experiences.

* * *

I have chosen to relate my learning experiences through anecdotes because my grandmother was a true educator. She made sure that every experience was a learning opportunity for me. She was a spirited teacher and had the appropriate verses, proverbs, quotes, Sanskrit slokas, chants and rhymes at her fingertips. She made sure that as a child, I learned as many sayings as I could.

She herself allowed reason to dictate and guide her life. She used her reasoning power to understand and look beyond the beliefs of the time. She was a true practitioner of science. The purpose of education was to understand life, understand the cause and effect behind everything, and to seek the truth. As an educated person, grandmother was very rational in her thinking. Education was meant to enlighten and awaken people about the truth.

Moola (birth star)

The following anecdote dates back to 1942–1943. I was born in January 1942. A cradle ceremony followed, where I was placed in a cradle and my name whispered in my ear. I was named Sujaya, Kusuma, and Ambuja. The priest prepared the horoscope, as was customary. Six months later, my father became very ill. Despite the timely medical care, his condition worsened, and he passed away at a very young age. Many relatives and friends came to pay their condolences.

Grandmother observed them and turned a blind eye to their ignorance and superstitions. Within six months, my 4-year-old sister suddenly died due to meningitis, even before she could be diagnosed! This was followed by my mother's death after an accident. Several relatives and friends came to pay their condolences. Among them, there were some women who made gestures at the baby, discussing the *Moola* that had uprooted the family.

Srirangamma ignored the women and returned with something in her hand. She called the ladies and led them to the back of the house, where bath water was heated in a hearth. She said in a calm voice, "Those of you who made such insensitive comments about the innocent infant, touch your hearts and feel how ridiculous your statements are. Here is the sheet where the Moola, which has caused our family this calamity, has been documented. Watch me get rid of it." She tore the horoscope and threw it into the hearth. "Now this Moola is *Nirmoola*, all gone. You are welcome to leave right now. You need not come back for the ceremonies. I have had enough of your condolences and sympathy. Thank you."

Srirangamma, who was made of different metal, could see that the innocent child had nothing to do with the tragedy, despite her intense grief.

This whole episode was narrated to me by my mother when I was old enough to understand.

* * *

The following anecdote dates back to 1948 and is titled *Amma Thayi*. All the primary school teachers in the zone were grandma's students at some time. Some of them would come home to clarify doubts or exchange notes.

Once, two teachers, Kumuda and Nagaveni, came home and asked me which class I was in. My friends Ramya and Rama were their daughters and were students at MLA School.

I had lost my birth parents as a toddler and was oblivious to this fact. I was raised by my grandmother. As far as I was concerned, my father's brother Kitta and Sarojamma were my parents. Their teenage children were my sister and brother, who doted on me.

I addressed my father as Peppa (*Periappa* in Tamil means Big Daddy). Since he was tall and handsome, I guess the name suited him.

I had lots of friends in school. Among them, Sudha was my best friend. Uma-Shashi, Rama and Ramya also played with me often. We ran around and played I Spy, and Catch-Catch. One day, three of my friends stood under a tree, whispered something and giggled! I asked them what they were laughing about. I wanted to laugh and have fun too. But, they acted unusually strange!

Then, Uma-Shashi shouted, "You go away, go away! You do not have a mother or father. You are an *Amma Thayi* (a beggar)."

I retorted immediately. "Why do you talk such nonsense? Of course, I have everyone in my family."

Again, one of them shouted, telling my classmates not to play with me because I was an *Amma Thayi*! By then, I felt rejected and hurt. I started walking, making my way home. As I walked, I started crying.

Sudha held my hand and gently said, "Don't cry, Suji. I'm your friend. I will always be your special friend."

Upon reaching home, I went straight to the swing and swung to console myself. I walked in, hugged my mother and cried. Grandma Amba said to me, "Come Suju, drink your milk."

"No Amba, I don't want milk."

"I have your favourite snack *Ksheera* for you"!

"I can't eat *Ksheera*, Amba."

"Will you sing and dance for me like you do every evening?"

"No, Amba, I cannot sing or dance."

She checked to see if I was feeling sick. I put my face on her lap and sobbed. Along with *Amma*, she kissed me goodnight and assured me that everything would soon be fine.

The next morning, when Amba wanted to braid my hair, I told her I did not want to go to school. I had a stomach ache. I sobbed and said, "I don't want to go to that school. They don't want to be my friends." I told her everything that had happened.

Amba spoke to her son Kitta and Amma. She assured me that everything would be fine. As we walked to school, I felt tall and strong as my parents held my hand. They met the Head Mistress, and with her permission they spoke to my friends, introducing themselves.

My father said, "Please come to our house to play on holidays. Then you can all meet Suju's family, play on the swing, and enjoy tasty snacks."

Grandma made a couple of trips to my school during the week. On Saturday, she had arranged a walking excursion to a building right behind our school, for the children and teachers of Class 2. She led the class to Seva Sadan, an orphanage. Our cook had brought fresh food on his scooter. My whole family was there, serving tasty Bisi Bele, Sweet Pongal, etc., to the 23 residents of Seva Sadan. My brother and sister served water and *papad*. I was allowed to serve the dessert, *burfi*.

Amba spoke to the Class 2 students and introduced the 23 residents of the orphanage as friends of Suji, who come home regularly to play and sing *bhajans*. She explained, "These children live here in this home with their aunties in charge. They have one or no parents. They go home once every two weeks to their grandmother, and return here."

The Class 2 students were also served some treats. Amba walked back to my school and spoke to the children and adults. "Sadly, the children in Seva Sadan have only one or no parents. Do you think they are all *Amma Thayis*? No! They live in their home and go to school.

The *Amma Thayis* you see on the streets, and at temples and bus stands are not bad, either. They do not hurt anyone. Some bad and greedy people force them to become *Amma Thayis* and beg because they don't have anyone to care for them." This is how Amba sensitised the Class 2 students to this issue.

Srirangamma also convened a follow-up meeting for all the teachers of young children and included Kumuda and Nagaveni as well. The agenda for the meeting was to sensitise teachers to be cautious of exposing young minds abruptly to information that they were not equipped to handle.

Kumuda and Nagaveni had obviously gone home and blurted out that Srirangamma's granddaughter had no parents, in the presence of their daughters.

* * *

This anecdote about the recycling of clothes and excesses dates back to 1954-1955.

I grew up with my sister's daughter Geeta in Kusum Bhavan, under the care of my parents and Amba. Geeta was about 7 years old, and I was 5 years older than her. Every Ugadi (New Year) and Deepavali, we would get new clothes. Amba taught us both a couplet by Sant Kabir Das.

Paani bhaade naav mein, (Just like when water starts getting filled in the boat,)

Ghar me baade daam, (and the house gets cluttered with valuable things like excess clothes furniture, utensils and footwear,)

Donon haath uleechiye, (join both hands to scoop up and give away, part with, and recycle,)

Yahee Sajjan kaa kaam. (this alone is the right thing for a wise person to resort to).

I first learned this couplet by heart, and slowly began teaching Geeta the same. Amba had taught us the meaning of every line of the poem. She initiated a routine for us, that of sorting our clothes and footwear two weeks before the festival. Venkatamma, our domestic help, would help us identify whatever we had outgrown. Of course, Geeta being younger, would inherit my lovely dressy long skirts.

On the following Saturday, Venkatamma and I would check if our piles of clothes needed mending, or if buttons needed to be replaced. I was encouraged to mend them with care. On Sunday, the clothes would be washed, dried and neatly folded. If Geeta or I wanted to keep a favourite apparel, Amba would allow us to keep it for a while. She would take us on a special trip to Seva Sadan to donate our clothes and footwear to our friends in need. Amba explained every line of the couplet and we understood the spirit of sharing and recycling.

We learned to enjoy recycling what we owned since our childhood because of Amba's influence. So, just before Ugadi and Diwali every year, it became a routine to make a special trip to Seva Sadan to donate our excesses to our friends.

I also learned to sew long and short skirts from Sarojamma, on the sewing machine. Amba would buy me enough fabric to sew clothes for children. A few months before Krishna Janmashtami, I would start sewing skirts for Geetha and her little sister Shashi, and also for our helpers' children.

On the fifth day after Krishna's birthday, our family would host an open-air *Baala Bhojan* on our terrace. All the children of Seva Sadan, our helpers' children, and children from the neighbourhood came home and enjoyed a feast. Our entire family served the young guests and gifted clothes to at least five of them.

We learned the joy of giving because of our family values.

Similarly, my birthdays were always an occasion to give, rather than to receive.

* * *

'A stitch in time, saves nine' dates back to 1952.

I wore my brand new beautiful, daily wear skirt. I loved the coloured floral design on it. I felt like a princess when I wore it. While playing in the garden, I was suddenly tempted to climb a tree. As usual, I told my grandmother of my plan. She advised that I should change into my old clothes, as the new dress might tear. Of course, I did not want to get out of my new favourite dress.

Sure enough, my red skirt got caught in a rough bark and it tore. I was very sad and scared as I went to Amba to report what had happened with tears in my eyes. Surprisingly, she was not angry. Nor did she scold me. With a small smile, she asked me to get the sewing kit that she had just bought me. I asked her why between sobs. She said that it was best to mend it right away! I did not want to do anything but cry for having torn my new apparel.

Amba pacified me as she stroked my back. "Well, it is torn. Now the only thing to do is to make sure that the tear does not get bigger. When it is all mended, you can continue wearing it every day. A stitch in time saves nine."

She instructed me to mend my beautiful dress with the back stitch and blanket stitch. As I completed mending my skirt, the tear was completely camouflaged. I was not only pleased that I could wear it again. I also learned that a stitch in time saved me from a bigger headache, that of mending a bigger tear! It had also mended my sadness upon having torn my new apparel.

Ever since then, every time I see a bedsheet, pillow cover, upholstery or dress, I remember the valuable proverb: A stitch in time saves nine.

As always, Amba's approach to life, her interactions and reactions were all amazingly educative and long-lasting.

* * *

The Treasure of Wealth That Multiplies As You Spend It!

(1956-1957)

My neighbour and dear friend, Devayani, was my senior. After completing her matriculation, she could not continue her schooling. Being the oldest daughter of 10 children from a humble background, she had to support her parents.

So, she chose to complete a teacher's training course from a private training centre so that she could be a nursery teacher. But the training course was conducted in English. Devi did not know enough English to understand or complete the coursework. Somehow, she felt confident that I could help her complete her training, even though I was just a teenager.

As I discussed the issue with Amba, she thought this would be a perfect opportunity for me to learn by teaching my dear friend. As always she quoted Kali Dasa's Sanskrit verse:

Na chora haaryam, [that which can never be stolen],

Nacha raja haryam, [that which cannot be confiscated by even a royal authority],

Na brathru bhajyam, [that which siblings cannot claim to share],

Nacha bhara kaari, [that which is not a burden to carry],

Vyaye Kruthe, vardhatha eva nithyam, [the wealth that multiplies everyday as you expend by teaching others]

Vidhya dhanam sarva dhana pradhanam. [such is the true treasure, the greatest of all wealth.]

Amba advised me to organise my own schoolwork and Devi's course work too. I took special permission to audit Devi's Saturday evening classes. I found that some of her curriculum was intimidating. Amba explained some of the concepts in Psychology and in child-rearing practices, as I was not mature enough to comprehend by just reading the text.

I continued teaching Devi regularly. Yet, she could not write the answers to questions. So she asked me to give her model answers too, which she would memorise. This was quite challenging for me as I had to prepare for my own finals too.

I somehow managed to help her because her course was divided into quarters. She had to sit for exams every three months. As she prepared for her exams, I was able to provide her the answers to the questions!

I felt proud when she passed her course and attended a job interview. When she got employed, my joy and Amba's pride knew no bounds. Our mission had been accomplished. I learned so much through this experience, and such learning is indeed doubled when you teach and help others.

* * *

Here is another anecdote of how Amba was a role model, who instilled the love of teaching and educating in others. Srirangamma died when I was in my early teens. There was so little that I could do then, to honour and acknowledge her for all that she had done in my childhood to prepare me for life.

Even as a youngster, I always aspired to be a teacher. Although I felt humble and shy to voice my desire, I had dreamed of starting a school when I grew up. I was fortunate enough that my dream came true. After specialising in Early Childhood Education in California, I pursued my Masters in Early Childhood Development and Early Childhood Education from M.S. University, Baroda. Subsequently, I worked as a Founder Teacher, doing spade work at a reputed school that was being established. The valuable experience of setting up the infrastructure, and planning a curriculum for a school without walls, prepared me to start my own special preschool on a part of my grandmother's property.

Kreedangana was established in 1981, as a school without walls, similar to Rabindranath Tagore's Santiniketan, with outdoor classes under trees! Eventually, I renamed it Kreeda Ranga (a stage for play) and dedicated it to my grandmother, Srirangamma. It was a great creative experience, and I was fortunate to be able to plan, develop, and work for the school for 35 years!

I was extremely fortunate to have the moral support and encouragement of my extended family and friends as I established and developed my preschool.

There was a child-friendly gazebo, where art classes were being conducted. This Octagonal shaped sit-out was dedicated to my mother Sarojamma who was an incredible art prodigy.

I must share my experiences in counselling to a few of our teachers and teenage staff. One of our young helpers suffered from vision impairment since her childhood. It was a challenge to help her undergo eye surgery at Narayana Nethralaya.

I was fortunate to be able to raise funds, counsel, negotiate and get another young woman's marriage conducted, after averting her attempt to commit suicide! Do you readers understand how my own life was enriched by educating little children, training teachers and other staff, counselling parents and participating in social work? I have felt blessed by dear Amba all along.

I learned several things, thanks to Amba who taught me about the various aspects of life and encouraged me in all my endeavours. Along with my mother Sarojamma, who also raised me, she contributed to my growth, maturity, and strength. She instilled her values in me and taught me to have faith in God and myself. There are plenty of mothers who nurture their children by feeding them. But these two special ladies fed my soul!

Exactly like King Midas's Touch, the touch of these two ladies made me blossom into a beautiful woman. I dedicate this book to B.A. Srirangamma, my Guru, who taught me everything that is there to be learned in a young girl's life.

This story of the immortal Teacher par Excellence, is far from over. This book is a tribute to an eternal teacher.

It lives on in believing in the the highest positivity and optimism, like that of Amba, my grandmother. Her life and spirit, continue to exist in trusting the ability to change the world's perception of women.

This is a tribute to the great lady, who lives for ever in the hearts of all that were touched by her iconic personality.

I hope that someday, a library can be set up in Amba's memory, to help teachers access books and periodicals. I'm also hoping that Srirangamma's Trust Fund which will be established from the proceeds of this book, will finance deserving students who respect, value and pursue a career in teaching.

Currently the process of setting up Ambil Amba Telang Trust is being planned in initiating a Trust Fund to the advantage of deserving teacher trainees.

* * *